SOUL REFLECTIONS TAROT

Sunshine Connelly

Artwork by Ana Novaes

SOUL REFLECTIONS TAROT

Copyright © 2025 Sunshine Connelly
Artwork © 2025 Ana Novaes

All rights reserved. Except for personal use, no part of these cards or this book may be reproduced, in whole or in part, without written permission from the publisher. These cards are for spiritual and emotional guidance only and are not a substitute for medical advice or treatment. The author's views, within and beyond this publication, do not necessarily reflect those of the publisher. We respectfully request that this content not be used to train AI-generative models or machine learning systems without the publisher's written consent.

Published by Blue Angel Publishing®
10 Trafford Court, Wheelers Hill,
Victoria, Australia 3150

info@blueangelonline.com
www.blueangelonline.com

Edited by Peter Loupelis and Jules Sutherland
Designed by Sunshine Connelly

Blue Angel is a registered trademark
of Blue Angel Gallery Pty. Ltd.

ISBN: 978-1-922574-40-4

Designed in Australia. Printed in China on sustainably sourced paper with soy-based inks.

Contents

Welcome - 9
The Tarot - 12
Using the Cards - 17
Reflection Questions - 34
Card Meanings - 36
About the Author - 280
About the Artist - 281

The Major Arcana

0. The Fool - 37	XI. Justice - 70
I. The Magician - 40	XII. The Hanged Woman - 73
II. The High Priestess - 43	XIII. Death - 76
III. The Empress - 46	XIV. Temperance - 79
IV. The Emperor - 49	XV. The Devil - 82
V. The Hierophant - 52	XVI. The Tower - 85
VI. The Lovers - 55	XVII. The Star - 88
VII. The Chariot - 58	XVIII. The Moon - 91
VIII. Strength - 61	XIX. The Sun - 94
IX. The Hermit - 64	XX. Judgement - 97
X. The Wheel of Fortune - 67	XXI. The World - 100

The Minor Arcana

The Suit of Cups:
Emotions and Feelings

Ace of Cups - 106

Two of Cups - 109

Three of Cups - 112

Four of Cups - 115

Five of Cups - 118

Six of Cups - 121

Seven of Cups - 124

Eight of Cups - 127

Nine of Cups - 130

Ten of Cups - 133

Page of Cups - 136

Knight of Cups - 139

Queen of Cups - 142

King of Cups - 145

The Suit of Pentacles:
Material and Earthly Matters

Ace of Pentacles - 150

Two of Pentacles - 153

Three of Pentacles - 156

Four of Pentacles - 159

Five of Pentacles - 162

Six of Pentacles - 165

Seven of Pentacles - 168

Eight of Pentacles - 171

Nine of Pentacles - 174

Ten of Pentacles - 177

Page of Pentacles - 180

Knight of Pentacles - 183

Queen of Pentacles - 186

King of Pentacles - 189

The Suit of Swords:
Intellect and Clarity

Ace of Swords - 194

Two of Swords - 197

Three of Swords - 200

Four of Swords - 203

Five of Swords - 206

Six of Swords - 209

Seven of Swords - 212

Eight of Swords - 215

Nine of Swords - 218

Ten of Swords - 221

Page of Swords - 224

Knight of Swords - 227

Queen of Swords - 230

King of Swords - 233

The Suit Of Wands:
Inspiration & Action

Ace of Wands - 238

Two of Wands - 241

Three of Wands - 244

Four of Wands - 247

Five of Wands - 250

Six of Wands - 253

Seven of Wands - 256

Eight of Wands - 259

Nine of Wands - 262

Ten of Wands - 265

Page of Wands - 268

Knight of Wands - 271

Queen of Wands - 274

King of Wands - 277

Welcome

Welcome to the *Soul Reflections Tarot* deck, your companion on a transformative path of healing, empowerment, and divine self-reflection. Anchored in the practice of Soul Mirroring, this deck opens a gateway for you to discover the profound truths within, through the world around us. Soul Mirroring accelerates personal growth by revealing how each encounter—be it with a person, situation, or fleeting thought—mirrors aspects of ourselves that call for attention, healing, or celebration.

This reflective practice encourages you to observe your reactions, emotions, and thoughts with detached compassion, recognising how energetic shifts from fear to love signal opportunities for evolution. It's a way of seeing with both your eyes and your heart, realising that the external world reflects our internal state. This realisation empowers us to transform fear into understanding and love, addressing the inner knots of discomfort that impede our spiritual and emotional wellbeing.

Recognising what is yours to heal and what isn't within your boundaries is key in this practice. Often, the healing or lesson isn't in the situation itself but in your reaction to it. Listen to your body's natural divination system to guide you, using these cards as a tool to help connect to self.

While channelling the universal Soul Mirror, I had deep insights into how we create our 3D reality. We use our mind's eye to project our inner energy into the world, including our cellular data. This projection, mostly subconscious, merges with the collective to shape our shared reality. Our bodies act as vessels, channelling through the heart and mind, as beautifully captured in the old saying: "We don't see things as they are; we see them as we are."

I feel deeply compelled to share this practical method of self-healing that has enriched my life in so many ways. This reflection practice has enhanced my connection with my inner being and accelerated my personal growth and self-healing. It has empowered me to take accountability for my life and the part of my consciousness that is intertwined with others, recognising and honouring the work necessary for our evolution. Now, more than ever, as we navigate this pivotal time in history, our inner workings are being brought to light in what I see as a continuous energetic inversion.

This deck is a powerful reminder of our inherent divinity and creative power. It challenges us to embrace our potential to heal, create, and transform our reality through love and intentional living. As co-creators, we hold the power to shape our experiences and uplift our collective consciousness, contributing to a world that reflects our highest selves.

As you work with these cards, you will learn to look beyond the surface. This process is not just about seeing the world differently; it's about coming back to *you*, rediscovering your truth, and embracing the transformative power of love and self-awareness. I welcome you to a mirror of seeing your true self, where every reflection, every card, brings you closer to the heart of who you are, who we are. Let us craft our lives as moving prayers, as art, as love — forever interconnected. May the world be your Soul Mirror.

With love always,
Sunshine

The Tarot

Tarot cards serve as a physical manifestation of your inner consciousness, allowing you to access the infinite wisdom that lies within. As you explore your inner world, you will discover a sacred space where your soul's essence is lovingly reflected, providing invaluable insights and guidance on your path to self-discovery.

The tarot deck comprises 78 cards, divided into the Major Arcana and the Minor Arcana, each card with its own unique meaning and symbolism. The Major Arcana, comprising 22 cards, represents the spiritual and karmic journey of life, touching upon universal themes and archetypes that mirror the human experience. From *0. The Fool*, signifying the beginning of a new journey, to *XXI. The World*, symbolising the completion of a cycle, these cards serve as guides on the path to personal growth.

The Minor Arcana, the remaining 56 cards, is divided into four suits: Cups, Pentacles, Swords, and Wands. These cards deal with the everyday aspects of life and delve into the emotional, material, mental, and creative realms.

The Major Arcana

The Major Arcana is the heart of the tarot deck, a collection of 22 cards that hold profound significance and represent the soul's journey through life. Each card embodies an archetype—a universal symbol reflecting the human experience—and serves as a guiding light for self-actualisation and spiritual growth. The Major Arcana cards weave a tapestry of life lessons that one encounters on the path to self-awareness.

The journey of the Major Arcana begins with the Fool, the embodiment of new beginnings, innocence, and potential. As the soul embarks on its quest, it encounters various archetypal figures, such as the Magician, who symbolises manifestation and personal power, and the High Priestess, representing intuition and the mysteries of the subconscious. Each card in the Major Arcana offers a unique lesson or insight, guiding the seeker through the complexities of life—both triumphs and setbacks—towards spiritual evolution.

The cards of the Major Arcana also encompass universal themes such as love, embodied by the Lovers, and transformation, as represented by Death. These cards not only reflect the individual's internal landscape but also resonate with the collective human experience, encouraging empathy, compassion, and understanding.

Ultimately, the Major Arcana serves as a mirror, reflecting the multifaceted journey of the soul and guiding us towards self-realisation and inner wisdom. These powerful cards provide a roadmap for personal growth, helping us navigate life's challenges with grace and resilience. By embracing the lessons and archetypes of the Major Arcana, we can deepen our connection to ourselves and the world around us, unlocking the infinite potential within.

The Minor Arcana

The Minor Arcana is the foundation of the tarot deck, consisting of 56 cards that delve into the intricacies of daily life and the myriad experiences that shape our personal journey. While the Major Arcana explores the spiritual and universal aspects of the human experience, the Minor Arcana offers insight into our emotions, relationships, ambitions, and challenges, serving as a compassionate guide through the ebbs and flows of life.

The Minor Arcana is divided into four suits: Cups, Pentacles, Swords, and Wands, each representing a distinct element and aspect of our existence.

Cups

- Associated with the element of water
- Speaks to our emotional realm
- Highlights matters of the heart, relationships, and intuition

Pentacles

- Connected to the element of earth
- Represents the material world
- Focuses on abundance, work, and the physical aspects of our lives

Swords

- Linked to the element of air
- Addresses the intellectual and mental realm
- Encompasses thoughts, communication, and conflict

Wands

- Aligned with the element of fire
- Delves into our creative and spiritual pursuits
- Illuminates our passions, ambitions, and personal growth

Each suit in the Minor Arcana progresses from the Ace to the Ten, followed by the court cards: Page, Knight, Queen, and King. The numerical cards reflect various stages or experiences within each suit's theme, while the court cards depict different aspects of personality, personal development, or the roles we play in life.

The significance of the Minor Arcana within the tarot deck lies in its ability to illuminate the subtleties and nuances in our daily lives. These cards offer a loving and empathetic perspective on the challenges we face and the triumphs we celebrate, helping us to better understand ourselves and others. By engaging with the wisdom of the Minor Arcana, we can embrace the complexities of life with compassion and grace, fostering a deeper connection with the world around us and our journey within it.

Using the Cards

Blessing the Cards

To begin your journey with tarot cards, establish a loving connection with your deck and ensure they are energetically protected. This creates a sacred space for you to access your intuitive wisdom and guidance and allows you to forge a deeper bond with your cards. By blessing and protecting your tarot cards, you show reverence for the powerful insights they can provide and cultivate an environment of trust, love, and respect.

Begin by finding a quiet space where you can sit comfortably and focus your attention on your deck. Close your eyes and take a few deep, cleansing breaths to centre yourself and relax all parts of your being. As you breathe, visualise a warm, loving energy enveloping you and your tarot cards. This energy serves as a protective shield, keeping away any negative influences and providing a safe space for you to work with your cards.

Next, hold your tarot deck in your hands and set a clear intention to bless and protect the cards. This reflects and expresses gratitude for yourself, as the cards are now an extension of expansive universal consciousness. Speak softly, either aloud or silently in your heart:

> *I call upon my guides, celestial beings, ancestors, and all those who love me unconditionally to envelop both me and my cards in their wisdom and warm, loving protection on this sacred journey. Together with love, divine light, and positive energy, we infuse these tarot cards, transforming them into a physical vessel for profound insight and transformative healing. May they guide me gracefully along the path towards my truest and most authentic self.*

Visualise a warm light infusing each card with loving energy. Imagine this light surrounding and permeating the entire deck, filling it with a sense of calm, protection, and positivity. As you do this, trust that your cards are now attuned to your energy and ready to guide you on your path.

Once you have completed this blessing and protection ritual, take a few moments to thank the Universe, your higher self, or any spiritual guides or deities you resonate with for their assistance and support. Gently wrap your tarot cards in a special cloth or store them in a dedicated pouch or box to maintain their energy.

By performing this loving ritual, you demonstrate your commitment to honouring the tool of tarot and your wisdom, creating a firm foundation for your personal practice. As you continue to work with your cards, remember to approach each reading with an open heart, allowing the guidance and insights to flow naturally.

Card Layouts & Spreads

The steps outlined below are a guide to support you in preparing and reflecting upon your readings. As you become more familiar and confident in your readings, you'll cultivate your own unique style and method. There is no incorrect way to approach tarot when you listen to your heart and follow its lead to reveal the path back to it — back to you.

Embrace your tarot experience and cherish the connection to your divine self, recognising the answers you seek reside within you. Tarot serves as a tangible extension of your consciousness, providing guidance and reflection on your journey. With pure and loving intentions, may you flourish and transform into the highest version of yourself, contributing to the elevation of our collective consciousness and fostering a world of greater understanding and harmony.

Prepare your space: Honour the time by finding a quiet, comfortable area where you can focus on your tarot reading and energy without distractions. You may wish to light a candle, burn incense, or play soft music to create a serene and calming atmosphere.

Centre yourself: Sit comfortably and take a few deep breaths. Focus on your breath and allow yourself to relax. Release any stress or concerns from your mind and be present in the moment.

Summon and protect: Close your eyes and set the intention to connect with your spiritual guides, angels, or ancestors who have your best interests at heart and love you unconditionally. Ask for their guidance, protection, and assistance in this reading. Also, invite your highest self to participate in this process, ensuring the wisdom you receive aligns with your soul's purpose.

Your question: Think about a specific question or concern you have, or simply ask for general guidance. Having an intention for your reading is important, even if it's broad and open-ended.

Shuffle and choose cards: Hold the tarot deck in your hands and focus on your question or intention. Shuffle the cards as you see fit, ensuring you infuse your energy into the deck. Connect and follow your intuition. When you feel the cards are adequately shuffled, you can choose a card (or cards) in various spreads and layouts — see below.

Interpret the card/s: Reflect on the imagery and symbolism of the card, considering how it relates to your question or intention. You may also like to consult the guidebook for additional insights into the card's meaning. Consider how the message from the card can apply to your life and think about the actions you can take based on this insight. Each card's entry in this guidebook contains questions to prompt practical self-reflection based on the card's meaning and message.

Give thanks: Be grateful for the wisdom and guidance you received from the tarot, your guides, and your highest self. Take a moment to reflect on the reading and consider how you can use this newfound knowledge, or different perspective, that you might not have initially seen without the connection.

One-Card Spread

The Soul's Mirror

The single-card spread invites you to shine a focused beam of light on a specific area of your life or a corner of your inner being that yearns for your attention. Ideal for daily contemplation or when your heart seeks clarity on a particular inquiry, this approach is beautifully simple yet profoundly insightful. The card you draw offers a beacon of guidance for the present moment and a question (or an answer) that weaves into the fabric of more complex spreads.

Each moment or situation holds within it the dual seeds of fear and love, challenging us to choose the path of positive action. Approaching the tarot with an open heart allows you to transmute fear into love, revealing the deep, innate wisdom that resides within. This loving practice assures you that solutions born of love are always within reach, encouraging a deep trust in the tarot's guidance and the wisdom of your inner self. Remember, a single card can whisper a question, sing an answer, or guide your steps through more intricate card spreads.

Follow the preparatory steps listed on the previous page. As you concentrate on your intention, draw one card from the deck using one of these technique.

- One way is to cut the deck into three parts moving from left to right, and then stack the piles back together in any order that feels right, choosing the top card as the answer.

- Another approach is to shuffle the cards and stop at a point to reveal the card that you have stopped at.

- You can also use the rainbow technique of laying the cards face down in a rainbow spread and feeling the cards with your hands to choose one from the deck.
- Sometimes while shuffling, a card might just jump out of your hands, which is an important card chosen for you!

After you have chosen a card, continue with the 'giving thanks' step described earlier.

Three-Card Spreads

Three-card spreads are versatile and insightful, serving as a go-to for clarity and guidance to navigate through life's layers. By drawing three cards, you can explore various dimensions — from the unfolding narrative of your personal journey from the past to the future, or delving into the interconnectedness of mind, body, and spirit. Whether you're reflecting on your life's journey, seeking solutions to current challenges, or aiming for inner balance, the three-card spread provides a straightforward, flexible framework for guidance and exploration.

Follow the preparatory steps described earlier. As you shuffle the cards, concentrate on your intention, and draw three cards from the deck. After you have drawn the cards, continue with the 'giving thanks' step described earlier.

Past–Present–Future

Card 1 symbolises the influences and lessons from your past that have shaped your current situation.

Card 2 illustrates your present circumstances, shedding light on the energies and challenges that you are currently facing.

Card 3 unveils the potential future outcome, providing guidance on your life's direction based on your current path and choices.

Situation–Obstacle–Advice

Card 1 reveals your current situation, providing insight into the circumstances and energies surrounding you.

Card 2 highlights the obstacles or challenges you may face, offering clarity on the factors that need to be addressed.

Card 3 presents valuable advice or guidance on overcoming these challenges and moving forward on your path.

Mind–Body–Spirit

This spread encourages a holistic approach to self-care and personal growth, promoting harmony and balance within your mind, body, and spirit.

Card 1 delves into the mental aspect of your life, shedding light on your thoughts, beliefs, and mental wellbeing.

Card 2 explores your physical state, providing insight into your body's health and vitality, and any areas needing attention.

Card 3 taps into your spiritual essence, revealing your soul's journey, inner wisdom, and connection to the Divine.

The Soul Mirror Spread

If you're using the *Soul Mirror Oracle* alongside this tarot deck, you'll find they complement each other perfectly, offering deep insights into a situation. Each card in the oracle deck encapsulates both fear and love states surrounding a central theme, presenting both a challenge and an avenue for positive action.

This spread clarifies the issue at hand and offers guidance on how to transcend it. Embrace this practice with a heart full of love, openness, and a readiness to discover and heal through the fears that confront you. Remember, the true key to unleashing your inner strength lies in navigating life's challenges with a spirit of love and a willingness to learn from every experience.

Follow the preparatory steps outlined at the start of this section. As you shuffle the cards, concentrate on your intention and draw one card from the *Soul Mirror Oracle* and two cards from the *Soul Reflections Tarot*, and place them in the positions shown in the diagram below. After you have drawn the cards, continue with the 'giving thanks' step outlined at the start of this section of this section.

Card 1 (from the *Soul Mirror Oracle*) is the central theme. It encompasses both the fear and love dynamics surrounding the situation and highlights the core issue or challenge you face while offering a broader perspective.

Card 2 (from the *Soul Reflections Tarot*) signifies the fear dynamic. It reveals the shadows, limiting beliefs, or challenges that hold you back in the context of the central theme.

Card 3 (from the *Soul Reflections Tarot*) signifies the love dynamic. It reflects the nurturing elements and generative beliefs that offer guidance towards an empowered resolution, illuminating the path to transcendence.

Five-Card Spreads

Theme Spread

The five-card tarot theme spread is perfect for those times when you crave a deeper understanding of your life's unfolding story or seek guidance on a specific question. This spread is a loving conversation with the Universe, offering a panoramic view of your current path, including the emotions, challenges, and potentials that lie ahead. It gently reveals the central theme of your inquiry, surrounded by insights into your present situation, the fears that may whisper to you, the challenges and solutions that await discovery, and the outcome that your actions and intentions are steering you towards. Let this spread be your beacon, empowering your reading with confidence and revealing the transformative power nestled within every challenge and question.

Follow the preparatory steps listed above. As you shuffle the cards, concentrate on your intention, draw one card and place it in the centre. Then, draw four more cards, placing them in a rectangle formation, with one card at each corner, as shown in the diagram that follows. After you have drawn the cards, continue with the 'giving thanks' step outlined above.

Card 1 represents the central theme of the spread.

Card 2 signifies the present situation.

Card 3 represents your fears in the context of the theme.

Card 4 signifies the challenges or the solution.

Card 5 suggests the possible outcome should the guidance be followed.

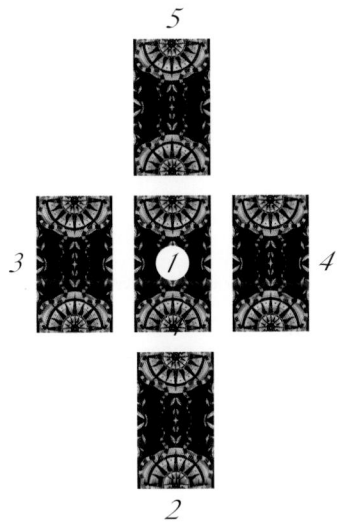

Five-Card Cross for Love

The five-card cross for love spread offers a profound exploration of the dynamics within your romantic relationship, making it the ideal choice for those seeking to deepen their understanding of love's complexities. This spread illuminates the heart of the matter, your perspective, your partner's view, the foundational influences of your relationship, and the potential future outcome. It's designed for moments when you feel the need to uncover the underlying themes and challenges shaping your connection with your partner. Whether you're navigating a specific issue, seeking to understand each other better, or contemplating the path your relationship is on, this spread provides clarity, insight, and guidance. It's a powerful spread for those wishing to look at their relationship as a mirror to themselves, with honesty, openness, and a desire for harmony and growth.

Follow the preparatory steps listed above. As you shuffle the cards, concentrate on your intention, draw one card and place it face down in the centre. Then, draw four more cards, placing them face down, as shown in the diagram below. Turn them over and continue with the 'giving thanks' step outlined at the start of this section.

Card 1 — Issue: signifies the present state or the issue between you and your partner.

Card 2 — You: symbolises your perspective on the situation.

Card 3 — Partner: represents your partner's perspective.

Card 4 — Influences: illustrates the foundation of the relationship or past influences contributing to the current issue.

Card 5 — Outcome: indicates the likely outcome or potential of the situation.

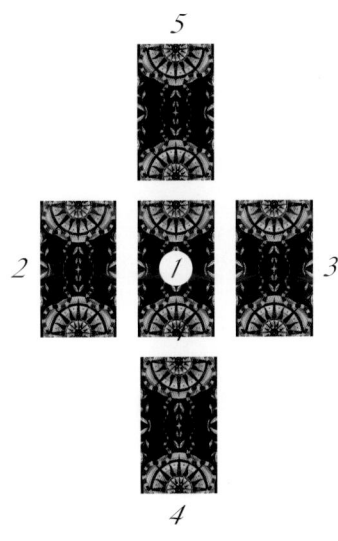

The Celtic Cross Spread

The Celtic Cross tarot spread unfolds as a deeply introspective reading, inviting you to mirror the soul's landscape against the backdrop of your life's intricate tapestry. This spread is particularly potent for those seeking to delve into the depths of their being, illuminating the present moment, discerning challenges, and uncovering hidden potentials through a lens of profound self-reflection.

This spread encourages a reflective exploration of various dimensions of your existence—highlighting the foundational influences that shape your path, the evolving dynamics of your past, present, and emerging future, alongside your inner perceptions and external reflections. Whether you're navigating personal dilemmas, relationship dynamics, career choices, or spiritual inquiries, the Celtic Cross spread offers a sanctuary for contemplation, empowering you with insights and clarity.

Follow the preparatory steps listed above. As you shuffle the cards, concentrate on your intention and draw ten cards, placing them in the order shown below. Then, continue with the 'giving thanks' step outlined at the start of this section.

Card 1 — Present: represents the current situation and the energies surrounding it.

Card 2 — Challenge: reveals the obstacles or challenges you may face.

Card 3 — Foundation: represents the underlying influences, past experiences, or events that have led to the present situation.

Card 4 — Past: shows the recent past and its impact on the current situation.

Card 5 — Possibilities: represents the potential outcomes or opportunities available.

Card 6 — Near Future: indicates the likely events or energies emerging soon.

Card 7 — Self-Perception: reveals how you perceive yourself in the situation and how it influences your choices.

Card 8 — External Influences: represents external factors, people, or energies influencing the situation.

Card 9 — Hopes and Fears: unveils your hopes, dreams, and fears related to the situation.

Card 10 — Outcome: indicates the potential outcome or final resolution of the situation based on your current path.

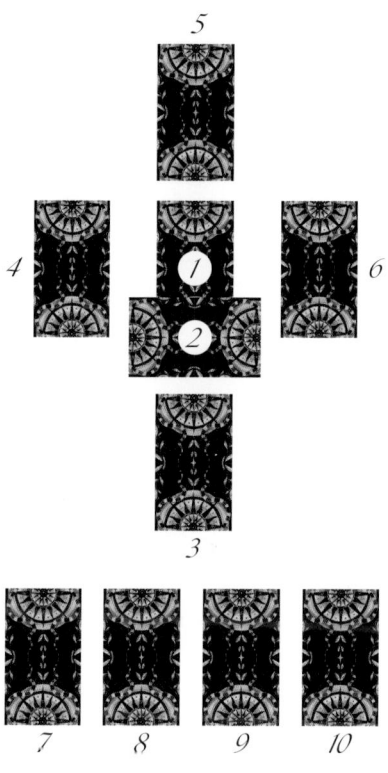

The Celtic Cross Spread

Reflection Questions

At the end of each card's message are some questions to help deepen your connection to the cards and enhance your readings. These questions are specifically designed to provoke thoughtful introspection, allowing you to delve further into the symbolism and messages hidden within each card and to understand what they may reflect or highlight about your current situation.

These questions serve as a practical tool for self-reflection and growth. They encourage you to explore the various dimensions of your inner world and examine the aspects of your life that require attention or change using the Soul Mirroring practice. By responding to these questions with honesty and vulnerability, you create a space for self-awareness and understanding to emerge. The insights you uncover through this process can empower you to make better decisions, improve your relationships, and align yourself more closely with your unique and authentic self. Use these reflection questions as a practical means of interpreting the cards and a vessel for transformation, spiritual growth, and deep healing.

It is my deepest wish that the reflection questions presented in this book serve as a beautiful reminder of the immense potential and power within you to create and shape your wonderful life. May they gently signal you to make the changes necessary to align with your most authentic self.

The Major Arcana

0. The Fool

Let go and embrace the opportunities of the unexpected!

New beginnings, taking risks, freedom, innocence, new path, spontaneity, opportunities

0. The Fool card invites you to embrace life with an open heart and mind, symbolising the start of a new journey filled with unexpected opportunities. Step out of your comfort zone and dive into the wild unknown. Life is full of infinite possibilities, and you are free to embrace them. Confront your fears and let go of the familiar with a light-hearted leap of faith. You are embarking on a new journey full of self-discovery, growth, and evolution, and by embracing change, you will truly realise your full potential through opportunities of the unexpected. Welcome the unknown with excitement and joy and know that the Universe is guiding you towards your greatest potential.

Reflection

How can I approach my experiences with a more open and curious mind and find new perspectives and opportunities for growth?

Can I approach my life with a sense of playfulness and joy and cultivate a childlike sense of wonder and curiosity about the world around me?

——— Reversed ———

Clinging to the familiar hinders growth and change.

Fear of change, insecurity, indecision, immature behaviour, irresponsibility, resistance

This card in reverse embraces the wisdom of uncertainty. In his contrary state, the Fool invites you to see the value in stepping out of your comfort zone as he dances on his head. It's an opportunity to recognise growth and learn from new experiences. Acknowledge your fear of the unknown as a signal of upcoming personal expansion and evolution. This card suggests the need to embrace life's unpredictable nature and find joy in the journey, even when the destination is unclear. It encourages you to see every unknown path as an adventure, a chance to discover more about yourself and the world.

Reflection

Consider the exciting opportunities that might lie in the realms of the unknown. How can stepping into uncertainty lead to greater self-discovery and personal growth?

Reflect on the potential for joy and spontaneity that comes with embracing new experiences.

I. The Magician

You have everything you need within to turn your ideas into reality.

Manifestation, ability, power, talent, transformation, resourcefulness

When *I. The Magician* is pulled from the deck, it speaks to the inherent magic and power within. You are a master alchemist, turning lead into gold by using the power of love, creativity, and your intuition. You can manifest your deepest desires and dreams simply by aligning your energy to your truth and love and releasing perceived limitations. Trust in your innate abilities and embrace the beauty of your unique gifts. The wand held by the Magician is a symbol of the power of the will, reminding you to channel and focus your energy and desires and trust in the journey of creation and manifestation. This is an invitation to embrace your magic, to believe wholly in yourself, and to take charge of your life with love, creativity, and intuition.

Reflection

What unique talents, skills, and abilities do I possess, and how can I use them to manifest my dreams and desires?

What limiting beliefs or patterns do I currently hold on to that may be blocking my ability to manifest my desires?

How can I approach my challenges and obstacles with creativity and resourcefulness, and use them as opportunities for growth and learning?

Reversed

Work through your creative blocks and communicate more effectively with your truth.

Deception, manipulation, lack of focus, scarcity of resources, miscommunication

Transform your challenges into creative power. In reverse, *I. The Magician* reflects a moment to reassess your connection with your inner talents and potential. It's a call to overcome self-doubt and to use your skills and resources creatively. This reversed card suggests a phase of recalibration, where you learn to align your intentions with your actions more authentically. It's a powerful mirror for recognising and breaking through self-imposed limitations, encouraging you to manifest your desires with renewed confidence and clarity.

Reflection

How can I turn obstacles into opportunities to showcase my creativity and resourcefulness?

What are my unique skills and talents? How might I use them more effectively to bring my dreams to fruition?

II. The High Priestess

Tune in to the whispers of your intuition and allow them to guide the way.

Intuition, mystery, inner wisdom, the Divine Feminine, all-knowing, higher power, clairvoyance

Embodying the essence of intuition, *II. The High Priestess* signifies inner wisdom and the mysterious forces that guide us from within. Tap into your divine feminine wisdom and embrace the power of the unknown. Take the time to slow down so you can hear the whispers of your soul. The High Priestess represents the power of receptiveness, the ability to be an open channel allowing the flow of knowledge to enter your consciousness. By embracing the energy of the High Priestess, you gain a greater understanding of yourself, the world around you, and the magic that lies within the mystery. There's a deep, untapped well of wisdom within you waiting to be discovered.

Reflection

In what way can I honour my inner voice and follow my own path, even if it goes against expectations or norms?

How can I cultivate a greater sense of balance and harmony between my inner and outer worlds?

What aspects of my life are currently calling for me to step into my power and claim my truth?

Reversed

Go inward to reconnect with your true being and resolve conflict.

Disconnection, blindness, clouded judgement, dishonesty, blockages, secrets

Use this time to reconnect with your intuition and inner wisdom. When *II. The High Priestess* appears reversed, it's a signal to delve deeper into your subconscious and intuition. It suggests a journey inward to rediscover your inner voice and truth. This reversal serves as a reminder of the power of self-awareness and the importance of listening to the whispers of your soul. It's an invitation to clear mental fog and seek clarity from within, illuminating your path with your own inner light.

Reflection

How can I reconnect with and honour my intuition?

What practices help me tune in to my inner wisdom?

In what ways can a stronger connection with my inner self guide me more clearly in my outer world?

III. The Empress

Tap into your creativity and bring abundance and prosperity into your life.

Creation, fertility, support, caretaking, the Divine Feminine, abundance, nurturing, luxury

When *III. The Empress* appears, it symbolises the embodiment of creativity, nurturing, and the abundant flow of life's gifts. Trust in the power of the feminine within. Allow yourself to be nurtured and embrace your own creative potential. In doing so, you will discover a deep and meaningful connection to the Divine and the ability to bring abundance and prosperity into your life and those around you. Trust in the goddess energy within you and utilise your inner resources to create a life filled with comfort and joy. The Empress is a symbol of the nurturing and supportive aspects of the feminine and a reminder that you have the power within to bring happiness and success into your life. It may also symbolise birth, whether that be a physical pregnancy or the birth of a new idea or project. No matter what lies ahead of you, take time to appreciate the beauty surrounding you.

Reflection

How can I nurture and care for myself and those around me and create a life of abundance and joy?

Can I deepen my connection to the world and honour its beauty and wisdom, using it to support my own growth and healing?

How can I approach my creative passions and pursuits with a sense of playfulness?

Reversed

Rediscover the abundance within.

Over-reliance, unproductive, idleness, external dependence, overbearing

The reversed Empress suggests a disconnection from your inner creativity and abundance, often leaning towards over-dependence on external sources for validation or support. Rediscover the abundance within and find a balance between nurturing yourself and others. This is a call to reconnect with your creative energies, to recognise the richness of your inner resources and harness this for yourself. This card mirrors the need to cultivate self-care and find joy in your own creative expressions. Take this as an opportunity to reassess how you can use your nurturing abilities to foster growth and abundance, both for yourself and in your connections with others.

Reflection

How can I balance caring for myself with caring for others?

What inner resources can I draw on to create more abundance and joy in my life?

IV. The Emperor

Lead with confidence and fairness and create a positive impact.

Authority, stability, structure, the Divine Masculine, leadership, responsibility

This card symbolises authority, stability, and the power of leadership rooted in wisdom. As you pursue your aspirations, let your ambition and determination propel you forward. Allow your natural authority and influence to create a secure and stable environment for yourself and those you cherish. This card serves as a gentle reminder to utilise your inherent skills and the power of your inner calm to bring order to chaos. The Emperor embodies wisdom and reminds you to take full responsibility and care for the empire you create. With confidence, lead with love and let your talents make a positive impact on your world and the collective experience of our reality.

Reflection

How can I use my innate leadership qualities and authority to inspire and uplift those around me and to create positive change in the world?

Can I approach growth and self-improvement with a sense of gentle encouragement and self-love?

What would best support me in achieving my goals, and how can I approach these with kindness?

Reversed

Invest time in nurturing your skills and emotional growth.

Immaturity, tyranny, indecision, inability, irresponsibility, ego, dominating

Cultivate your leadership skills through the practice of self-awareness. When reversed, *IV. The Emperor* highlights areas where your leadership and decision-making skills can be improved through open and honest self-reflection. It's an opportunity to grow in maturity, responsibility, and self-discipline. This card invites you to explore ways to balance authority with empathy and to develop a leadership style that is both strong and compassionate. It's a call to introspection, to understand the roots of any dominance or rigidity, and to transform them into wisdom and balanced power.

Reflection

What is my current approach to leadership and control?

How can I bring more emotional intelligence and fairness into my decision-making?

Consider how self-awareness can lead to a more fulfilling and effective leadership style.

V. The Hierophant

Live a life guided by your wisdom and higher purpose.

Faith, spiritual wisdom, traditions, education, teaching, blessings, inner peace

Embrace the balance between the material and spiritual aspects of your life with the guidance of *V. The Hierophant*. This card reminds you to find inner harmony before seeking it in the world around you, for your inner world is reflected in your outer experience. If facing inner challenges, turn to a trusted mentor for guidance and wisdom. This is a time of new beginnings, where you will be blessed with knowledge and spiritual transformation. You may also find yourself passing on your own knowledge and teachings, whether consciously or not. Embrace this journey with an open mind and heart, and allow yourself to blossom into the best version of yourself through this transformative inner journey.

Reflection

What role does tradition and ritual play in my life?

How do these practices help me feel connected to my community, my ancestors, or my beliefs?

Am I currently living in alignment with my highest values and beliefs?

Reversed

Break free from conventional thinking in pursuit of finding your truth.

Rebellion, new methods, challenging, individuality, non-conformity, originality

In their contrary form, *V. The Hierophant* encourages you to challenge conventional wisdom and explore new perspectives in your quest for truth. This reversal highlights a period where traditional beliefs or established methods may no longer serve your journey towards self-discovery and personal growth. It invites you to question the status quo and to consider what unique and original paths might lead you closer to your authentic self. This card is a call to embrace your individuality and trust in your inner guidance, even if it means breaking away from societal norms or expectations. It's an opportunity to redefine what spirituality, faith, and wisdom mean to you on a deeply personal level. By daring to walk your own path and honouring your unique insights and experiences, you pave the way for a more fulfilling spiritual journey and allow others to do the same.

Reflection

In what areas of my life am I following conventions that don't align with my true self?

How can I courageously pursue my own path and express my individuality?

VI. The Lovers

Welcome divine love and soul connection into your life.

Union, divine love, soulmate, relationships, romance, connection, harmony

Open your heart fully to the power of love and experience the joy, passion, and beauty that it brings. Whether you seek a new romance, a deeper connection with your partner, or a stronger spiritual connection with yourself, *VI. The Lovers* is a reminder to allow love to flow through you and enhance and amplify your desires. Cherish the relationships in your life, including the one with yourself. You are whole, and your relationships are here to elevate you in love, not complete you. Embrace the mindset of compassion and understanding as you navigate any difficult challenges you might be experiencing. See them as divine learning experiences for soul expansion and growth. Bask in the glory of love, and trust the Universe is bringing you all the joy and happiness you could ever imagine.

Reflection

In what ways do I currently experience love and connection in my life? What can I do to strengthen and deepen these relationships?

How do I currently approach my own personal growth and self-love?

In what ways can I cultivate a deeper sense of self-awareness and self-acceptance?

Reversed

Embrace introspection and healing to transform relationship challenges.

Conflict, imbalance, detachment, separation, arguments, conflict, lack of trust

In its reversed position, *VI. The Lovers* signifies a time to contemplate the less harmonious aspects of your relationships. It may reflect conflicts, miscommunications, or a sense of detachment, urging you to explore these challenges as mirrors of your inner world. This period is not just about external discord but more about recognising and addressing the internal misalignments these conflicts reveal. This message calls for introspection into how your fears, insecurities, or unresolved issues might reflect in your relationships. Examine the roots of any discord and understand your role in these dynamics. This introspective journey heals and realigns yourself and those around you. Rather than viewing these challenges as obstacles, see them as opportunities for growth and deeper understanding.

Reflection

How are the conflicts or challenges in my relationships mirroring my internal struggles?

What lessons can I learn from these experiences to foster growth and understanding?

VII. The Chariot

With determination and willpower, you will achieve success!

Determination, control, willpower, movement, victory, progress, direction

A powerful card, *VII. The Chariot* represents success, willpower, and determination. You have the strength and control to achieve anything you set your mind to. Trust your abilities, as they will overcome any obstacle in your path. You can inspire and motivate others and, in turn, spread the positive energy of success to others along the way. Whether you are chasing a personal goal, embarking on a new venture, or taking charge of a situation, *VII. The Chariot* encourages you to move forward with confidence and love. Remember to celebrate milestones along the way, for the journey is just as much a victory as the outcome. Success isn't just about reaching the finish line but about the progress you make and the lessons you learn along the way. Embrace the road ahead!

Reflection

Am I currently feeling a sense of direction and purpose in my life, or do I feel lost and uncertain?

What steps can I take to clarify my goals and create a clearer vision for my future?

What practices or activities help me to feel centred and focused, and how can I use these to ignite my inner flame?

Reversed

Trust in your ability to overcome any obstacles.

Lack of direction, obstacles, impatience, self-doubt, giving up, indecision

When *VII. The Chariot* appears reversed, it suggests a period of stagnation or uncertainty, where obstacles seem to hinder your progress and cloud your sense of direction. This reversal calls for deep reflection on the internal barriers and doubts that mirror these external challenges. Recognise the greatest battles lying within — overcoming these will lead to a renewed sense of control and direction in your life. By embracing the lessons of this reversed card, you learn to trust in your ability to navigate through obstacles, using them as stepping stones rather than stumbling blocks. It's an opportunity to cultivate patience, reassess your goals, and find new ways to move forward with clarity and confidence.

Reflection

In what areas of my life am I experiencing resistance or obstacles, and how can these guide me towards growth and realignment?

How do my internal doubts and fears reflect in these external challenges?

How can I transform impatience and indecision into strength and determination?

VIII. Strength

You are capable of taking on any challenge with grace.

Courage, inner strength, gentle power, compassion, grace, endurance

This card symbolises the quiet power of courage, compassion, and inner resilience. You are a powerful force to be reckoned with, and you have the resilience and determination to overcome any challenge that comes your way. When you face adversity, trust in yourself and your abilities and have faith that you will emerge stronger and more empowered on the other side. Strength also comes in the form of patience, kindness, and compassion. As you move forward on your path, trust in the wisdom of your inner lion and allow its bountiful and fearless energy to guide you towards your dreams. With grace, resilience, and unwavering determination, you can achieve anything you set your mind to.

Reflection

When facing challenges or obstacles, how do I typically react?

How can I cultivate more self-control and resilience in the face of difficulty?

What fears or self-doubts am I currently struggling with, and how can I tap into my inner strength and courage to overcome these challenges?

Reversed

You have the power to overcome any obstacle.

Inadequacy, insecurity, self-doubt, lack of confidence, fear or anxiety

When *VIII. Strength* is reversed, it reminds you to face and embrace your inner vulnerabilities. Your feelings of inadequacy, insecurity, or self-doubt reflect deeper issues needing attention and compassion. This period calls for introspection, urging you to explore the roots of your perceived weaknesses and understand how they mirror aspects of your inner self. True strength lies in acknowledging and working through vulnerabilities, not just in outward force. Engaging in this reflective process allows for transforming feelings of inadequacy into opportunities for self-empowerment. It's a time for practising self-compassion, challenging self-doubts, reaffirming your worth, and developing a stronger sense of self-belief and inner resilience. This card encourages you to use current challenges as stepping stones to cultivate greater emotional strength and courage.

Reflection

In what ways do my insecurities and fears mirror deeper aspects of myself that need attention and care?

How can I practise self-compassion to overcome feelings of inadequacy or lack of confidence?

IX. The Hermit

The answers you seek lie within you.

Solitude, introspection, reflection, inner guidance, wisdom, contemplation, analysis

Guided by your inner wisdom and intuition, *IX. The Hermit* appears from the deck offering an invitation to embark on a journey of self-discovery. Take a step back from the noise and distraction of the external world and turn your attention inward to reconnect with your inner being. The Hermit is a wise and compassionate guide, offering support and mentorship as you navigate through the darkness and confusion to find your way back to the light. It's a reminder that you already have all the answers and knowledge you need within you; trust your inner guidance and truth. Gift yourself time and self-compassion as you reconnect to the divine wisdom within you and assess any decisions. When you feel ready, move forward with a loving heart, trusting that your inner guide will illuminate the path.

Reflection

What am I currently seeking outside of myself?

How can I seek to understand or learn through introspection and reflection of the external world?

Can I incorporate the lessons I've learned during my period of solitude into my life?

Reversed

Take time to reconnect with your inner wisdom.

Isolation, loneliness, disconnection from self, impatience, external validation

Reversed, *IX. The Hermit* encourages you to recognise feelings of isolation, loneliness, or disconnection from your inner self as signals to reconnect. This card reflects a tendency to seek answers or validation externally, urging you to turn inward and trust your intuition. It's a call to pause and reflect on why you might be relying on external sources for guidance rather than tapping into your own deep well of knowledge. This period is about understanding the value of your inner voice and the power of self-reflection.
It invites you to embrace solitude, not as a state of loneliness but as a powerful tool for reconnection and introspection. By acknowledging feelings of impatience or the need for external validation, you can begin to foster a deeper, more meaningful relationship with yourself.

Reflection

How can I redirect my search for guidance inward?

What steps can I take to strengthen my connection with my inner wisdom?

In what way can I create space for solitude and introspection in my daily life?

— X. The Wheel of Fortune —

Embrace the continual turning of the wheel of life.

Destiny, life cycles, luck, karma, fortune, destiny, sudden change, unexpected events

When *X. The Wheel of Fortune* appears in your reading, it is a sign that you are in a transition or turning point in your life. This card is a loving reminder that life is full of ups and downs and that every experience, good or bad, can offer valuable lessons and opportunities for growth and healing. Trust that the Universe is guiding you towards your highest good and that everything is happening for a reason. As a co-creator of life, the transformation you once called upon is now unfolding, guided by the Universe's hand. Be gentle with yourself, and trust in your own inner strength and resilience during transitions. Even in times of challenge, there is always the potential for positive change and new opportunities, new ways to grow and evolve. Embrace the turning of the wheel with an open heart.

Reflection

How do I respond to unexpected events or changes in my life?

Am I open to new experiences and opportunities, or do I resist them out of fear?

How can I cultivate a greater sense of inner peace and resilience during times of change and transition?

Reversed

You hold the power to break free from negative cycles.

Setbacks, bad luck, resistance, repeating patterns, stagnation, inflexibility

When reversed, *X. The Wheel of Fortune* highlights how setbacks or feelings of 'bad luck' often mirror internal resistance to change or a clinging to outdated beliefs and behaviours. Recognise and break free from negative cycles and stagnant patterns that may impede your growth. You are encouraged to see these challenging times not as misfortunes but as reflections of what you need to reassess or let go of in your life. This is a powerful moment for self-reflection, understanding that you hold the key to changing your trajectory. By embracing flexibility and openness to change, you can turn the wheel in your favour, transforming what appears as misfortune into valuable lessons and opportunities for personal evolution. This reversal is an empowering reminder that even in times of stagnation, you possess the ability to initiate meaningful change and steer your life towards a more fulfilling path.

Reflection

What repeating patterns or resistances am I currently facing, and how can they guide me towards positive change?

How can I adopt a more flexible and open-minded approach to the unexpected events in my life?

In what ways can I actively participate in changing my current circumstances to align with my desired path?

XI. Justice

Everything will be truthfully seen.

Fairness, justice, balance, equality, honesty, integrity, legal matters, accountability, truth

Eyes closed to avoid bias, *XI. Justice* represents truth, fairness, and the balance that comes from honouring integrity and accountability. You are a powerful agent of change, with the ability to bring balance and fairness into every aspect of your life. By embracing the principles of honesty, integrity, and accountability, you make clear and rational decisions reflecting your values and aligning with your highest good. The Universe supports your commitment to doing what is right, and your actions will have a positive impact on those around you. By cultivating a deep sense of self-awareness and a compassionate attitude towards yourself and others, you can embody the principles of fairness and equality in your life. Trust your own moral compass and your ability to make a positive difference in the world. You have the power to create a life that is grounded in truth and guided by love.

Reflection

How have I been holding myself back from fully expressing myself, and what steps can I take to release these self-imposed limitations?

In what ways can I align my actions and decisions with my core values and beliefs to live a more authentic and purposeful life?

Reversed

You have the power to right the wrongs.

Injustice, dishonesty, imbalance, unfairness, legal matters, corruption, no accountability

The reversed version of *XI. Justice* is a call to confront and rectify any areas of injustice, dishonesty, or imbalance in your life. It reflects situations where fairness and integrity may be lacking, either within yourself or in your external experiences. This reversal invites you to examine how these themes are mirrored in your own actions and beliefs. It encourages a deep self-assessment of where you may not be holding yourself or others accountable or where you might be contributing to a sense of unfairness or corruption, whether consciously or unconsciously. This is an opportunity to realign with your core values and principles, ensuring that your actions and decisions embody honesty and justice. It's a powerful reminder that you have the strength and moral fortitude to right the wrongs you encounter and to contribute positively to your world.

Reflection

In what areas of my life do I need to foster more honesty and fairness?

How can I hold myself and others more accountable to ensure justice and integrity?

XII. The Hanged Woman

This pause is necessary to gain new insights.

**Surrender, let go, sacrifice, patience, perspective,
new insights, pause, contemplation**

Hanging from the tree of life, *XII. The Hanged Woman* symbolises the need for surrender and the patience to gain fresh perspectives. This moment of suspension allows you to release what no longer serves. Take this opportunity to tune in to your inner wisdom and connect with your intuition. Use this time of stillness to gain a deeper understanding of yourself and your place in the world.
By embracing this moment of surrender, you open yourself up to new perspectives and insights that will benefit your life's journey. True power lies in the willingness to let go and release control.

Trust the process, even when it feels uncertain or uncomfortable. Have faith that everything is unfolding exactly as it should. You are exactly where you need to be.

Reflection

What steps can I take to tune in to my inner wisdom and connect with my intuition, even in moments of busyness or chaos?

How can I surrender to the flow of life, trusting that I am exactly where I need to be?

Reversed

Embrace transformation and release your resistance.

Resistance, indecision, stagnation, delays, victim mindset, stubbornness, disinterest

This card in reverse indicates a period where indecision, stagnation, or a victim mindset may be prevalent, reflecting an inner struggle against necessary change. Actively embrace transformation and release any resistance that hinders your progress. It calls for a shift in perspective, urging you to let go of stubbornness and disinterest in your personal evolution. Examine areas where you are clinging to outdated beliefs or fears, preventing you from moving forward. Growth often requires leaving your comfort zone. Delays in this process can be a form of self-sabotage. By recognising and addressing these resistances, you open yourself up to new opportunities and a renewed sense of purpose. The reversal of *XII. The Hanged Woman* is a call to action, encouraging you to actively participate in your own transformation and embrace the changes life brings with a sense of openness and curiosity.

Reflection

Where am I resisting change in my life, and what fears might be fuelling this resistance?

How can I shift my mindset to view change as a positive and necessary part of growth?

What steps can I take to move past indecision and embrace the transformations awaiting me?

XIII. Death

Let go of what no longer serves you.

Big transformations, change, new beginnings, endings, rebirth, evolution, liberation

In tarot, *XIII. Death* holds a sacred and transformative energy, inviting you to surrender to the wisdom of life's natural cycles. As you release what no longer serves you, you energetically create space for new beginnings and a deeper alignment with your soul's path. The endings you are experiencing, and the shedding of old patterns and beliefs, lead you towards inner growth and evolution. As you embrace the power of change, let go of any resistance or fear that holds you back and allow yourself to be born again. Deeply honour the sacredness of this moment, and trust you are exactly where you need to be right now. With each self-restricting release, you make room for more joy, abundance, and love to enter your life.

Reflection

What old patterns or beliefs am I ready to shed to make space for new growth and evolution in my life?

In what way can I embrace the power of change and see endings as opportunities for transformation and rebirth?

What new possibilities and opportunities am I excited to welcome into my life as I release what no longer serves me?

Reversed

Trust in your ability to embrace transformation.

Holding on, rigidity, fear, resistance to change, stagnation, avoidance, blockages

This card in reverse suggests a reluctance to accept change, driven by fear or resistance. Holding on to outdated patterns or avoiding necessary endings is causing stagnation and blockages in your life. Reflect deeply on why you might resist the natural flow of endings and new beginnings; confront and release the fears binding you to the past. This card reminds you that transformation is integral to life's journey, and clinging to what is familiar hinders your growth and evolution. Embracing change, although challenging, is vital for your personal development and the realisation of your true potential. The reversal of *XIII. Death* encourages you to let go of the old to make way for the new, trusting this process of renewal will lead to great fulfilment and liberation.

Reflection

What am I holding on to that is no longer serving my highest good?

How can I address and release my fears related to change and transformation?

In what ways can I encourage myself to be more open to the process of letting go and embracing new beginnings?

XIV. Temperance

Balance and self-discipline bring inner harmony and growth.

Harmony, balance, moderation, healing, patience, peace, alchemy, higher purpose

This card symbolises the importance of balance, patience, and the harmonious integration of all aspects of yourself. You have the power to create a life that honours your highest self and supports your soul's growth and continuous transformation. By finding and maintaining a state of flow that integrates all aspects of yourself, you will experience the inner peace and clarity that comes from aligning with your truth and purpose. Embrace life's pleasures and challenges in moderation, and trust that you can navigate its ebbs and flows with grace and ease. Through the practice of temperance, you can access the wisdom and guidance of the Universe to bring your sacred purpose and dreams to life.

Reflection

How can I bring more balance and harmony into my life by embracing moderation and flow?

In what ways can I practise self-discipline and patience to support my growth, transformation, or healing?

How can I approach life's challenges and pleasures in a way that honours my highest self and supports my inner peace?

Reversed

Address imbalances with courage and find renewed energy.

Disharmony, imbalance, excess, impatience, lack of moderation, confusion

In reverse, *XIV. Temperance* calls for a courageous examination of imbalances, excesses, or impatience in your life. It indicates a period of disharmony or confusion, signalling the need to reassess and recalibrate your approach to achieving balance and inner peace. It is an invitation to reflect on areas where you may be overindulging or lacking moderation and consider how these behaviours disrupt your sense of equilibrium. Face these challenges with honesty and determination, and recognise that true harmony is achieved through conscious effort and self-awareness. By addressing these imbalances, you open the door to a renewed sense of energy, clarity, and purpose. The path to balance and fulfilment often involves making adjustments and cultivating patience and discipline, leading to a more centred and aligned existence.

Reflection

In what areas of my life do I need to restore balance and moderation?

What steps can I take to cultivate a more harmonious and balanced lifestyle?

XV. The Devil

Consciously free yourself from negative influences.

Temptation, addiction, materialism, obsession, shadow self, manipulation, greed

Lurking mysteriously in the shadows, *XV. The Devil* represents the need to confront and free yourself from the negative patterns and influences that hold you captive. Delve into the depths of your being and engage with the inner demons that hold you back from living a life of true freedom and fulfilment. We are complex beings with both light and shadow within us; by acknowledging and integrating all aspects of ourselves, we can achieve a state of wholeness through reflection and understanding. Although *XV. The Devil* can be a daunting card—associated with temptation, addiction, and fear — it is also a powerful symbol of the human capacity for transformation and transcendence. Acknowledging your life lessons and facing your fears unlock the chains of self-imposed limitations, to then be liberated to access a deeper level of self, authenticity, and freedom.

Reflection

How can I turn the lessons into a source of empowerment and growth and use them to deepen my connection with my inner truth?

What can I draw upon to help me in my journey towards greater self-awareness and liberation?

In what way can I learn to embrace the complexity of my own nature, including my shadow self, and use it as a source of insight for healing and development?

Reversed

The decision you need to make will be easier than you think.

Freedom, release, detachment, liberation, overcoming addictions, transcendence

The reversed version of *XV. The Devil* suggests an impending ease in making decisions that will lead to freedom, detachment, and liberation from negative influences. This position signifies a turning point where the grip of temptation, addiction, or material obsession begins to loosen, offering a clearer path towards overcoming these challenges. The struggles you've faced are about to become more manageable, indicating a shift towards greater self-awareness and control. Recognise and release the self-imposed chains, whether they be unhealthy habits, toxic relationships, or limiting beliefs. This is a powerful moment of realisation that the power to transcend these bonds lies within you. Embracing this period of liberation allows you to step into a more authentic and empowered version of yourself.

Reflection

What steps can I take to further detach myself from negative influences and addictions?

How can I reinforce my newfound sense of freedom and self-control?

In what ways can this period of liberation and transcendence help me grow and evolve as a person?

XVI. The Tower

Trust that chaos will bring powerful transformation.

Sudden change, disaster, upheaval, destruction, chaos, divine intervention, revelation

Pulling *XVI. The Tower* from the deck suggests sudden upheaval and the inevitable transformation that follows. Amid chaos and destruction, hold grace and trust in the divine process unfolding because the upheavals are paving the way for a deeper revelation of your truth. Allow the force of divine intervention to shatter illusions and break down what no longer serves your highest good. Surrender to the currents of change that are reshaping your life. You are being called to let go of what doesn't serve you, trusting that the Universe is creating space for something better to emerge. Through this process, you have the opportunity to discover a newfound sense of strength, courage, and resilience. This card doesn't signify a punishment but an invitation to rebuild your life with greater authenticity, alignment, and purpose. Trust the human vessel keeping you afloat — you are being ushered to a place of liberation and inner peace.

Reflection

What do I need to let go of to rebuild my life on a foundation of truth and alignment with my highest good, and how can I take action towards that goal?

What hidden truths or revelations are being brought to the surface through the upheavals in my life, and how can I embrace them as opportunities for personal healing, growth, and expansion?

Reversed

Break down the barriers and open the doors to your truth.

Avoidance, fear of change, repression, self-deception, incomplete cycle, hiding from truth

In reverse, *XVI. The Tower* signifies a crucial moment for breaking down internal barriers and opening the doors to your deeper truths. It points to a tendency to avoid necessary changes, repress emotions, or engage in self-deception, which hinders your personal growth and keeps you in incomplete cycles. Confront your fears of change and upheaval; face the truths you may be hiding from. This is an invitation to examine the foundations of your beliefs and behaviours, identifying and dismantling those that no longer serve your highest good. By bravely addressing these issues, you create the opportunity for profound transformation and the emergence of a more authentic self. The reversal of *XVI. The Tower* reminds you that sometimes the most significant growth occurs when you are willing to let go of old structures and bravely embrace the new and unknown.

Reflection

What internal barriers am I currently upholding that prevent me from embracing change and growth?

How can I confront and overcome my fears and self-deceptions to allow for personal transformation?

XVII. The Star

A brighter and more hopeful future awaits.

Guidance, hope, renewal, inspiration, positivity, healing, inner peace, rejuvenation, health

The essence of *XVII. The Star* symbolises hope, renewal, and the promise of a brighter future. You are a divine being of light, filled with infinite hope, creativity, and grace. The Universe is guiding you towards a path of healing and renewal, so trust the wisdom within you and the signs shown to you externally. Take time to nurture yourself and bask in the glow of divine, infinite love and light. Believe in yourself and the power of hope to bring about positive change and transformation in your life. You are a radiant star, so shine your light and share your unique gifts with the world.

Embrace the limitless possibilities available to you and allow yourself to be filled with a sense of wonder and magic.

Reflection

What new opportunities or paths of growth are currently emerging for me, and how can I align with my inner guidance to move towards them with confidence and clarity?

Can I nurture my own light and inner radiance and share my unique gifts with the world in a way that brings joy and fulfilment to myself and others?

Reversed

Stay open to new possibilities, even in moments of disconnection.

Disconnection, insecurity, lost, disappointment, depression, uncertainty

Appearing reversed, *XVII. The Star* still shines down on you, inviting you to stay open to new possibilities and maintain hope, even in moments of disconnection, insecurity, or uncertainty. This phase is characterised by feelings of confusion, disappointment, or depression, indicating a temporary detachment from your inner light and guidance. It's a call to rekindle your faith in the Universe and yourself, recognising that these periods of disconnection are also opportunities for deep introspection and re-evaluation of your path. *XVII. The Star* encourages you to seek and embrace new perspectives and sources of inspiration, even when they seem obscured by current challenges. Find the light within the darkness, maintain hope when the path ahead is unclear, and trust that this period of uncertainty is necessary for your journey towards growth and enlightenment. Every setback or moment of doubt can lead to a renewed sense of purpose and a deeper connection with your true self.

Reflection

How can I find hope and inspiration during times of disconnection or uncertainty?

What steps can I take to reconnect with my inner guidance and sense of purpose?

XVIII. The Moon

*Take note of your intuitive messages
and dream meanings.*

**Illusion, intuition, subconscious, dreams, cycles, deception,
the unseen, hidden, fear**

In the deep and mysterious realms of *XVIII. The Moon*, you are being guided through the unknown. Let go of the illusion of control and allow yourself to surrender to the ebb and flow of life. In the darkness, there is stillness and space for deep introspection, where you can connect with your inner wisdom and intuition. Let go of fears and doubts and energetically create space for the magic of the unknown. You are being called to embrace your feminine energy and trust in your intuition as you journey towards your innermost being. All will be revealed in divine timing. For now, let the gentle light of the moon nurture and hold space for your deepest fears and secrets, transforming them into illuminating wisdom.

Reflection

What intuitive nudges or inner whispers am I receiving, and how can I honour and follow them even if they challenge me?

How can I cultivate a sense of mystery and wonder in my life and allow myself to embrace the unknown with curiosity and excitement rather than fear?

Reversed

Let go of fears and illusions to gain clarity and insight.

Release, clarity, letting go, confrontation, overcoming, understanding, awakening

The reversed energy of this card symbolises the release of fears and illusions, allowing for greater clarity and insight. Step into a period of awakening, where you are invited to examine and release the subconscious fears and doubts distorting your perception of reality. Embrace this opportunity to dispel the shadows of confusion by shining a light on them, bringing a deeper understanding of yourself and your circumstances. This reversal is about moving beyond the surface level of situations, tapping into a more profound and authentic level of intuition and insight. It's a call to trust your inner guidance and navigate uncertainties, recognising that the journey to truth often involves confronting what has been hidden or repressed. Reversed, *XVIII. The Moon* reminds you that every challenge of understanding is an opening for personal growth and enlightenment.

Reflection

What fears or illusions do I need to release to better understand my situation?

In what ways can confronting my subconscious doubts lead to greater self-awareness and insight?

XIX. The Sun

You are radiating pure light, confidence, and abundance.

Joy, vitality, success, positivity, confidence, innocence, abundance, wholeness, presence

Allow the radiant warmth of *XIX. The Sun* to embrace you with love and positive energy, reminding you of the endless possibilities that exist within your reach. You are surrounded by an abundance of joy, success, and prosperity, and every step you take towards your dreams will be met with positivity and reward. Trust your inner light and let it shine brightly, illuminating your true path and guiding you towards new opportunities for growth and expansion. Let go of any doubts or fears that hold you back and step forward with confidence, knowing you are surrounded by love and support every step of the way. The world is waiting for you to share your light!

Reflection

What does success mean to me, and how can I work towards achieving it right now in a way that aligns with my inner being?

How can I embrace my unique talents and gifts and share them with the world in a way that brings me fulfilment and happiness?

What brings me joy and positivity in my life, and how can I cultivate more of it?

Reversed

Take small steps each day to embrace your inner light.

Potential, sadness, delay, burnout, inner child, scarcity, overlooked, disconnection

The reverse of *XIX. The Sun* suggests a phase where your radiance is dimmed, perhaps due to burnout, scarcity, or feeling overlooked. Reconnect with your inner child and the simple joys that ignite your spirit. Find and celebrate the small yet significant successes in your daily life, reminding you that each step, no matter how small, is a step towards embracing your full potential. In this period of perceived scarcity or delay, there lies an opportunity for introspection and re-evaluation of what truly brings you joy and fulfilment. The light within you is always present and waiting to be expressed, even if it requires patience and persistence to shine through the clouds of temporary challenges.

Reflection

What small steps can I take each day to reconnect with and embrace my inner light and joy?

How can I nurture my inner child and find fulfilment in simple pleasures?

What can I do to stay hopeful and positive, even when facing challenges or delays in my journey?

XX. Judgement

Step into a new chapter of your life with clarity and self-forgiveness.

Awakening, judgement, transformation, clarity, self-evaluation, revelation, purpose

The appearance of *XX. Judgement* reminds you that you have the power to transform your past experiences into something beautiful by embracing forgiveness, renewal, and spiritual awakening. Take a loving and honest look at yourself and your life. Trust your strength and wisdom, see the beauty and potential within, and let go of old patterns that no longer serve you. As you reflect on your journey, let your heart guide you towards your inner truth and deepest desires. Let go of the judgement and criticism that hold you back and look towards the freedom and liberation that comes from self-awareness and self-acceptance — your own unique unfolding of you and your life's creation.

Reflection

What patterns or behaviours no longer serve my growth and transformation, and how can I release them with compassion, forgiveness, and gratitude?

Can I honour my past as a version of myself that brought me here — and embrace this new chapter with gratitude, joy, and a renewed sense of purpose?

Reversed

It's time to let go of your old self and step into the new version of you.

Self-doubt, resistance, fear of change, stagnation, avoidance, self-punishment

The reversed form of *XX. Judgement* is a potent reminder to let go of self-doubt, resistance, and fear of change, urging you to step into a new, more authentic version of yourself. It highlights a period where stagnation, avoidance, or self-punishment holds you back from embracing the transformation awaiting you. This reversal calls for a deep and compassionate self-examination, encouraging you to release the old patterns and limiting beliefs that no longer serve your highest good. Trust the process of renewal and believe in your capacity for growth and change. By shedding the layers of your old self and embracing the journey of evolution, you open yourself to new possibilities and a life aligned with your divine purpose.

Reflection

What fears or doubts prevent me from embracing change and growth?

How can I release the aspects of my old self that no longer serve me?

What steps can I take to move forward with confidence and trust in my journey of transformation?

XXI. The World

Bask in your well-deserved success and completion.

Wholeness, completion, accomplishment, integration, fulfilment, totality, travel

In tarot, *XXI. The World* signifies completion and accomplishment, representing a significant milestone in your life. It reminds you that you have integrated all aspects of yourself and are now in a state of harmony and wholeness. Having achieved your goals, you are ready to celebrate your success. Revel in the totality of your being, and honour your connections with others. You have the power to manifest your dreams and share your gifts with the world. You are an empowered and enlightened individual, and this card affirms that you are ready to take on whatever comes next with love and a sense of purpose and fulfilment.

Reflection

What successes or challenges am I particularly proud of, and how have they shaped my personal growth and development?

What new possibilities and opportunities are opening to me now that I've completed a chapter of my journey?

Reversed

Embrace the changes needed to achieve your goals and fulfil your true potential.

Incompletion, dissatisfaction, unresolved issues, unachieved goals, disharmony

The reversal of *XXI. The World* represents an opportunity to reassess and adjust your path to align with your deepest aspirations. Embrace the necessary changes and actions to achieve your potential and complete the goals you've set for yourself. The journey towards completion is often nonlinear and requires continuous self-reflection and adaptation. It's a time to confront any unfinished business or lingering doubts and take proactive steps towards creating the fulfilling and harmonious life you desire. This is not a sign of failure but rather a nudging call to action, urging you to persevere and continue striving towards your ultimate vision.

Reflection

What areas in my life feel incomplete or unfulfilled, and what steps can I take to address these?

How can I realign my actions and goals to reflect my true aspirations more closely?

What changes or adjustments are necessary for me to achieve a greater sense of harmony and completion in my life?

The Minor Arcana

The Suit of Cups
Emotions and Feelings

The suit of Cups beckons us to explore the **depths of our emotional landscape**, encouraging us to listen to the whispers of our hearts. In the practice of Soul Mirroring, this suit serves as a reflective pool, mirroring the **emotions present** in our external experiences as a guide to what needs attention within our internal world. By embracing the lessons held within the waters of our feelings, we foster personal growth and deepen our connection to the universal sea of emotions that binds us all.

Ace of Cups

Overflowing with love and beautiful new beginnings.

New beginnings, love, fertility, creativity, fulfilment, renewal, awakening

The *Ace of Cups* overflows with the purest love and emotional fulfilment. Trust the Universe's abundant blessings and open your heart to fully receive them. If you are working on a new project, let your creativity flow from the depths of your being, and it will flourish and bring you great joy. This card also strongly indicates a significant new relationship, pregnancy, or other important emotional event in your life. Positive emotions flow within and around you, along with a deep sense of peace and harmony. Bask in this wondrously abundant time!

Reflection

How can I open my heart and allow more love and emotional fulfilment into my life?

In what ways can I express my creativity and tap into my intuitive side to bring more joy and fulfilment into my work?

How can I approach new beginnings with a sense of openness and receptivity, trusting in the Universe's abundance and love?

Reversed

Recognise and release emotional blockages and open your heart to receive.

Blocked emotions, repression, unfulfilment, disconnection, emptiness

The *Ace of Cups* in reverse is a sign that your heart may be experiencing blockages or repressions, leading to feelings of unfulfilment or disconnection. Take a moment to pause and reflect on your emotional wellbeing. Recognise these barriers and gently release them. It's an opportunity to explore what may be causing a sense of emptiness or a disconnect from your emotional self. By acknowledging these challenges, you can open your heart to healing and transformation. Embrace this period as a necessary step towards rediscovering your capacity for love, creativity, and joy. Remember, every empty cup has the potential and capacity to be refilled with new, nourishing experiences and emotions. Open your heart to receive!

Reflection

What internal barriers might prevent me from experiencing emotional fulfilment, and how can I dismantle them?

How can I create a safe space for myself to explore and express my emotions, even those that are challenging or uncomfortable?

Two of Cups

Rise together in love.

Partnership, love, connection, harmony, mutual attraction, unity, romance, commitment

The *Two of Cups* is a sacred symbol of a profound emotional bond with another that is founded upon mutual love, respect, and shared values. True love starts with self-love, and by nurturing yourself first, you attract relationships that honour and reflect your best self. Have faith that the Universe is conspiring to bring you a partner who will walk alongside you on your journey, supporting and helping you grow into the highest expression of yourself. Embrace this divine connection with an open heart and allow yourself to receive the unconditional love you deserve.

When dealing with toxic relationships or co-dependency, trust that you can set healthy boundaries for your growth and evolution. You are worthy of deep and fulfilling connections that uplift and raise you in love.

Reflection

How can I cultivate self-love and self-acceptance, recognising my own inherent worthiness and deservingness of deep and fulfilling relationships?

How can I create healthy boundaries and communicate these, along with my needs, clearly and lovingly?

What can I do or say right now to raise my partnership in love?

Reversed

Align with your true being to attract the right relationships.

Discord, imbalance, broken relationship, misaligned values, disconnection, betrayal

The *Two of Cups* in reverse calls you to a deeper understanding of your inner world and its impact on your external relationships. It highlights the presence of discord, imbalance, or misalignment in your current connections, stemming from broken trust or differing values due to mixed communication from within. Reflect on the importance of aligning with your true self to attract the right relationships into your life. This card encourages introspection and honesty about whether your connections are based on mutual respect and shared values. Misalignments are opportunities to reassess and realign. See the discomfort of disconnection or betrayal as gateways to personal growth and clear communication, not as obstacles. Restore balance within yourself, which in turn, reflects your external relationships. Embrace this period as a transformative journey towards understanding your true relationship needs and desires.

Reflection

How can I align more closely with my true self to ensure my relationships reflect my values and needs?

In what way can I improve my communication within to express my needs better and give myself a framework (or boundaries) in my external relationships?

Three of Cups

Embrace and celebrate the joy of connection.

Celebration, friendship, socialising, support, community, teamwork, collaboration

The *Three of Cups* radiates with the warmth of love, connection, and sacred friendship. You are never truly alone in this world — there is a loving, supportive community surrounding you, ready to share in your joys and sorrows. Embrace the spirit of teamwork and consider the potential of working on a project or idea with aligned connections. Allow yourself to fully immerse in the experience of togetherness and trust the power of shared creativity and collaboration to bring about something truly magnificent. Your tribe is there to lift you up, inspire you, and offer a helping hand whenever needed. So, take a leap of faith and allow the collective energy of your community to guide you forwards.

Reflection

How can I cultivate deeper, more meaningful connections with those around me?

What are some ways that I can share my joy and celebrate the achievements of others? What steps can I take to create a supportive and value-aligned community around me?

Reversed

Create space for new, more aligned connections.

Disconnection, gossip, isolation, betrayal, selfishness, lack of support, abandonment

The *Three of Cups* in reverse signals a period where feelings of disconnection, isolation, or even betrayal might be prevalent. Take the time to reflect on the nature and health of your social connections. It encourages you to identify and move away from relationships that no longer align with you, either characterised by gossip, selfishness, or lack of support. In doing so, you create space for new, more honest connections that truly resonate with your values and aspirations. Consider the quality of your interactions and the impact they have on your wellbeing. Embrace self-care and self-awareness, recognising that stepping back from unfulfilling social situations is sometimes necessary for personal growth. Don't worry about how this will unfold with the current unhealthy connections, as they too will feel something is misaligned and may also not resonate with your energy. Let this special time be a transformative one, where you reassess your social circle and consciously choose who you want to share your energy and the creation of your life with.

Reflection

What signs indicate a social connection may not be healthy or beneficial for me?

In what way can I actively seek out and nurture relationships that are more aligned with my true self and values?

Four of Cups

A period of stillness will offer you the clarity you seek.

Introspection, stillness, healing, self-compassion, acceptance, clarity, renewal

The *Four of Cups* invites a period of stillness and introspection, offering you the clarity you seek. Through this period of contemplation and stillness, create a sacred space to connect to your innermost being, and explore the parts of yourself that need healing and attention. In this process of self-reflection, approach yourself gently, with compassion and self-love. Rather than judging yourself for your shortcomings or perceived failures, choose to embrace your imperfections and see them as opportunities for growth and learning. By nurturing yourself with kindness, you will overcome negative self-perceptions, and emerge with a renewed sense of clarity, acceptance, and gratitude. Allow yourself to sink into a state of restful contemplation, and trust that this journey of self-discovery will lead you towards healing, self-awareness, and renewed positivity.

Reflection

Why am I feeling discontented, and how can I explore these feelings in a loving and compassionate way?

What areas in my life need greater attention or healing, and how can I prioritise these with self-love and gentleness?

Reversed

Approach life with a renewed sense of positivity.

Gratitude, awareness, clarity, re-engagement, renewal, positivity, inspiration

When the *Four of Cups* is reversed, it signifies a time where the flow around you has stopped, and you risk living in a stagnant state. Awaken from the stillness and re-engage with life with a renewed sense of positivity and awareness. Shift your physical body and mindset, recognising that every moment of apathy or discontentment has been a stepping stone towards clarity and gratitude. Step out of the shadows of self-reflection and into the light of active participation in the world around you. You have an opportunity to be inspired and to inspire others, to see the beauty in the mundane. Move your body to move your energy and thoughts, and approach every experience with a sense of wonder and enthusiasm. As you reawaken to the possibilities of life, allow yourself to be filled with a renewed sense of hope, creativity, and an eagerness to embrace new opportunities. This is a moment of transformation, where your inner journey begins to manifest outwardly, bringing forth a brighter, more vibrant and refreshed version of yourself.

Reflection

In what way can I transform my recent reflections and realisations into positive actions and attitudes?

How can I foster a sense of gratitude for the lessons learned during periods of contemplation?

Five of Cups

Allow yourself to let go and accept what cannot change.

Disappointment, grief, sorrow, turmoil, defeat, regret, failure, hardship

The *Five of Cups* highlights the emotional weight of loss and the need for emotional healing. During moments of disappointment and heartbreak, it is crucial to be kind to yourself. Allow yourself to acknowledge and honour your emotions without allowing them to consume you. These emotions are signals from your innermost being, guiding you towards your highest self. Celebrate your awareness of them and appreciate the empowerment of this self-awareness. Life is a journey filled with peaks and valleys, and every experience presents an opportunity for healing, growth, and transformation. Embrace the challenges with a compassionate heart, and trust your ability to overcome them. You possess a strength and resilience that deserves recognition and self-love. Let this love guide you towards inner peace, happiness, and healing.

Reflection

How can I use my past experiences to grow and transform?

How can I practise self-compassion and extend kindness to myself during moments of heartbreak and adversity?

Reversed

Pick yourself up and move towards a brighter future.

Acceptance, moving on, forgiveness, release, renewal, learning, resilience

The *Five of Cups* reversed symbolises resilience in the face of adversity, and the ability to learn valuable lessons from your experiences. This is your moment to rise from the ashes of past sorrows and embrace the path of healing and renewal. It beckons you to practise acceptance and forgiveness, both for yourself and others, as a means of releasing the burdens of the past. It is a powerful reminder that every ending paves the way for new beginnings. As you let go of regret and disappointment, you make room for hope, growth, and new opportunities. Embrace this phase of your life with an open heart, and trust your innate capacity to heal and prosper. Allow yourself to be inspired by the endless possibilities ahead, and step into a future where you are stronger and wiser.

Reflection

What steps can I take to forgive myself and others and let go of past hurts? How can my past disappointments be transformed into sources of strength and learning?

In what ways can I actively seek out new opportunities and experiences to aid in my journey of renewal and resilience?

Six of Cups

Cherish the sweet memories of the past, as they offer gifts for the present.

Childhood, nostalgia, innocence, memories, past, sentimentality, reunions

Memories from the past offer valuable lessons that shape your present and future. Allow yourself to connect with the innocence and joy of your childhood and recognise how those moments formed a foundation for who you are today. Use the wisdom and insights gained from your past experiences to navigate the challenges of the present and guide you towards a bright future. In this moment of reflection, acknowledge any emotional baggage weighing you down and preventing you from moving forward.

Allow yourself to fully experience those feelings and then release them, making space for growth and transformation. Be mindful of patterns or habits keeping you stuck in the past and be willing to let go of what no longer serves your highest good. Every moment offers an opportunity for learning and transformation; have faith in your ability to navigate the challenges of life with love and grace.

Reflection

What joyful memories from my past can I draw inspiration and guidance from in this moment?

How do I cultivate a sense of playfulness and curiosity in my life?

What lessons have I learned from my past that help me navigate present challenges with greater wisdom and clarity?

Reversed

Release any emotional baggage from your past that may be holding you back.

Naïvety, stuck in the past, stagnation, grudges, baggage, neglect

The *Six of Cups* reversed invites you to release any emotional baggage from your past that holds you back. Recognise areas where you might be naïvely clinging to the past, perhaps due to unresolved feelings or grudges. Gently let go of what no longer serves your growth and free yourself from the weight of old baggage. By doing so, you avoid stagnation and open the doors to personal development and new experiences. This reversal also speaks to the importance of acknowledging and healing any neglect or hurt carried over from your past. Break free from the chains of old patterns and embrace the present with a clear and open heart. As you let go of these burdens, you make room for joy, growth, and fresh opportunities in your life.

Reflection

What aspects of my past am I holding on to that prevent me from fully embracing the present?

How can I acknowledge and heal from past hurts in a constructive and compassionate way?

In what ways can I actively move forward, leaving behind unhelpful patterns and embracing new opportunities for growth and happiness?

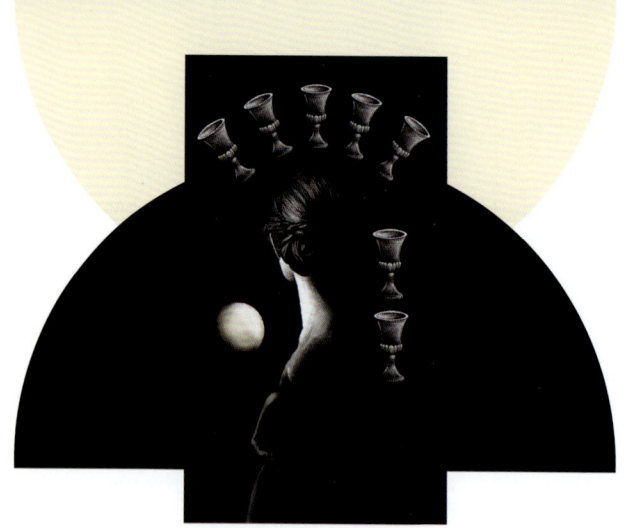

Seven of Cups

Explore your options, and choose the path that truly aligns.

Choices, options, fantasy, imagination, temptation, illusions, dreams, ambition

The *Seven of Cups* represents countless possibilities that lay before you, with the Universe ready to support you in manifesting your deepest aspirations. In the midst of these options, stay anchored in your heart and trust your inner wisdom to guide you towards what truly matters. Instead of being overwhelmed by illusions or distractions, prioritise self-love and inner alignment as you discern which path most accurately connects with your truth. By listening to your heart and taking focused steps towards your dreams, you can create a life full of abundance and joy that truly reflects who you are. Embrace the power of your imagination, trust in yourself, and believe that the Universe is conspiring to help you achieve your highest potential. Remember to stay grounded and nurture the magic of possibility within and around you.

Reflection

How can I stay grounded and realistic while still holding space for my dreams and desires?

How can I let go of illusions and distractions that hold me back and trust in my inner wisdom to guide me towards what truly matters?

What dreams and possibilities excite me the most, and how can I take grounded steps to bring them to life?

Reversed

Release the illusions and distractions that have held you back.

Clarity, focus, realism, rationality, grounded, discerning, realisation

The *Seven of Cups* in reverse signifies an important shift from dreaming and contemplating to achieving clarity and focus. It invites you to sift through the illusions and distractions that have previously clouded your judgement. Embrace realism and rationality, and identify what is truly attainable and aligned with your deepest values, even in tiny steps. This reversal encourages you to take a grounded approach to your aspirations, urging you to discern which of your many dreams are most feasible and meaningful. By releasing fanciful or unrealistic expectations, you pave the way for genuine realisation and achievement, first in baby steps, then in leaps and bounds! Embrace this newfound clarity to make choices that are well-informed and deeply connected to your authentic self. This is a time to let go of what is unattainable or misleading and focus your energy on goals that are within your grasp and resonate with your inner truth.

Reflection

What illusions or unrealistic expectations do I need to let go of in order to move forward more effectively?

How can I cultivate a more rational and grounded approach to my choices and aspirations?

Eight of Cups

Release what no longer serves you and embark on a transformative journey.

Letting go, moving on, transition, abandonment, release, discontentment, detachment

When the *Eight of Cups* appears, it suggests you are about to walk a profound journey of inner exploration and self-discovery, guided by the transformative power of letting go. Release anything that no longer resonates with your soul, including relationships, beliefs, and habits that have become unhealthy or out of alignment. This process of release may bring up deep emotions and fears but trust that you have the courage and strength to work through those knots to unveil your true, radiant being on the other side.

As you journey towards the unknown, recognise you are guided by the infinite wisdom of your heart and the Universe, which is always conspiring in your favour. Letting go creates space for new experiences, opportunities, and connections that are projected into the world from your deepest desires. May this journey be one of self-discovery, self-love, and growth as you trust in the infinite potential of your spirit.

Reflection

What aspects of my life am I ready to release in order to make space for new growth and opportunities?

How can I approach transitions and changes in my life with curiosity and openness rather than fear and resistance?

Reversed

Find closure and move towards greater fulfilment.

Fear of change, resistance, stagnation, attachment, avoidance, repression

The *Eight of Cups* reversed addresses our common tendency to resist or shy away from life transitions, a pattern of behaviour that leads to stagnation or creates an unhealthy attachment to what once was. It is a gentle nudge, urging you to seek closure and overcome the fear of change. Confront and let go of any lingering fears or suppressed emotions impeding your progress. Embrace change, even when it feels daunting, recognising that each step taken is a stride towards greater fulfilment. This reversal emphasises the necessity of processing unresolved issues and emotions, thus allowing you to close one chapter of your life with confidence and step forward into the next. Acknowledge the futility of trying to control the uncontrollable and release any unrealistic hopes of altering the past. Focus instead on what you can influence. As you achieve closure, a profound sense of release will envelop and hold you, paving the way for new possibilities, growth, and an inner peace permeating from within.

Reflection

What am I holding onto that is preventing me from moving forward, and how can I begin to let it go?

What steps can I take to actively seek closure in areas of my life that feel unresolved or stagnant?

Nine of Cups

Your deepest wishes and desires are manifesting into reality!

Satisfaction, happiness, pleasure, gratitude, abundance, wishes granted, success

Your wishes and desires are manifesting, bringing a sense of fulfilment and joy into your life. Connect with the abundance and joy surrounding you, knowing your deepest wishes are being realised. Immerse yourself completely in this feeling of satisfaction, letting it permeate your being and saturate you with a sense of peace and contentment. Celebrate your successes and trust that every step and hardship you have faced has led you to this point. Honour the interconnectedness of all things and allow yourself to feel gratitude for the people and experiences that have brought you to this moment. Embrace the present moment with an open heart and allow yourself to be guided towards your next steps with a sense of ease and flow. Let this moment be a reminder of the power of inner healing and manifestation, and let your heart continually be your compass as you continue your soul journey.

Reflection

What past experiences have brought me to this moment of attainment, and how can I honour and appreciate them?

In what way can I continue to connect deeply with my heart and intuition in order to guide me towards the next steps on my journey of growth and expansion?

Reversed

True abundance comes from within first.

Unfulfilled, discontentment, overindulgence, disappointment, lack, greed, emptiness

This card reversed brings to the surface the profound truth that genuine abundance originates from within. It invites you to introspect and confront any feelings of discontentment or emptiness hidden beneath the surface. Steer clear of overindulgence and greed, as these often represent misguided attempts to fill an internal void. Dive deeper into your inner world, exploring what truly brings you satisfaction beyond material or external achievements. Reassess your values and discover contentment in the simplicity and authenticity of your true self. In doing so, you cultivate an internal sense of abundance independent of external factors, leading to a more balanced and rewarding life. Embrace the journey of self-discovery and tap into the deep well of joy residing within you. Your external world will naturally align with this inner state as you do so.

Reflection

In what areas of my life do I feel unfulfilled, and how can I address these feelings internally rather than seeking external solutions?

How can I cultivate a sense of inner abundance and satisfaction, independent of material possessions or external validation?

Ten of Cups

Complete emotional fulfilment and contentment.

Harmony, happiness, family, love, celebration, fulfilment, unity

In the radiant light of the *Ten of Cups*, embrace the harmonious symphony of connection and love in your life. United, you and your loved ones create a sanctuary of joy, a sacred space where you can all flourish, learn, and grow. Through the mirror of your connections, self-reflection accelerates growth and healing as you uncover hidden truths and gain profound insights from the shared experiences or insights reflected upon you. Embrace these relationships as catalysts for transformation, learning from both the beauty and the challenge, ultimately fostering a deeper understanding of yourself. Cherish the moments of togetherness, for they are the nourishing waters that sustain your soul and empower you to grow, evolve, and share your light with the world. This card is a wonderful indicator of prosperity and abundance.

Reflection

What actions can I take to cherish and celebrate the joyous moments of togetherness in my life?

In what ways can I contribute to the creation of a nurturing and loving atmosphere that encourages mutual growth and understanding with my loved ones?

Reversed

Healing through understanding can restore the bonds of love and harmony.

Disconnection, disharmony, family discord, broken relationships, dissatisfaction

In its reversed position, the *Ten of Cups* reveals a period of disconnection or disharmony, especially in close relationships or family dynamics. However, this card also serves as a powerful reminder that unity has the transformative ability to turn chaos into an oasis of love and fulfilment. Actively work towards healing broken relationships and resolving dissatisfaction. Open up to understanding different perspectives and actively bridge gaps formed over time. This presents an opportunity to cultivate your needs and desires through newly created lines of open communication, forgiveness, and a deeper emotional connection. Embrace this challenge as a journey towards restoring harmony and rediscovering the joy of togetherness. By fostering an environment of love and mutual respect, you transform a discord of instruments into a harmonious and symphonic unity, strengthening the bonds that tie you to your loved ones.

Reflection

What steps can I take to heal disconnections and disharmony within my personal relationships?

In what way can I contribute to creating a nurturing and loving atmosphere that encourages reconciliation and mutual satisfaction?

Page of Cups

Let your open-hearted curiosity lead you on an abundant voyage.

Imagination, creativity, intuition, curiosity, sensitivity, innocence, inspiration, openness

Embrace the tender spirit of the *Page of Cups* as you venture into the depths of self-discovery, guided by your curiosity, intuition, and limitless creativity. Let your heart guide you, allowing the wisdom of your emotions and the transformative beauty of vulnerability to shape your journey. Open yourself to any possibility and let your imagination be a beacon of light, guiding you to deeper connections, spiritual growth, and your true potential. Listen deeply to your heart's messages and trust that it speaks from all facets of your being — from your inner child to your wise old soul. Open fully to the treasures of your multidimensional, creative being.

Reflection

How can I tap into my imagination and create a guiding light for my journey towards self-discovery?

How can I listen deeper to my heart's messages and trust the wisdom that emerges from my creative inner child or my wise old soul?

Reversed

Reconnect with your creative essence to guide you.

Insecurity, blocked creativity, emotional immaturity, distraction, self-doubt

This card reveals that insecurity, distraction, or self-doubt may block your creative flow. Confront and let go of any fears or doubts that dampen your creative energy because it's the perfect time to try something completely different. Seize this chance to evolve and refine your creative abilities. Ponder what may be causing these creative obstacles, then guide yourself back to your inspiring, artistic flow. Transform these blockages by shifting your mindset and actively engaging in creative activities. When you do, clarity and emotional insight will follow. This period marks a reawakening to the delights of creative exploration guided by your intuition. By facing and conquering these inner barriers, you pave the way for a more enriched and satisfying creative journey where you can express your authentic self freely and confidently.

Reflection

What specific fears or doubts hinder my creativity, and how can I address them?

How can I nurture my emotional growth to support my creative expression?

In what ways can I reconnect with my inner creative spirit and allow my intuition to guide my artistic endeavours?

Knight of Cups

Decide based on how you feel rather than what you think.

Romance, charm, imagination, idealism, creativity, artistry, graceful, dreamer

The *Knight of Cups* invites you to lead with your heart, letting emotions and intuition guide your decisions. Set forth on a heart-centred journey infused with passion, imagination, and tender resilience. Let love, creativity, and spiritual evolution illuminate your way, forging genuine connections with your soul that those around you will mirror. Surrender to the guidance of your intuitive heart and embrace the dance of life and the transformative power of emotional vulnerability through lessons, healing, and shared experiences. Trust your innate capacity to manifest your dreams, weaving together a world where love, inspiration, and soulful nourishment flourish.

Reflection

In what way can I harness my gentle strength to navigate life's challenges?

How can I embrace vulnerability and emotional expression to create a deeper understanding of myself and others?

Reversed

Transform disappointments and insecurities into opportunities for growth.

Disappointment, jealousy, escapism, insecurity, unreliability, stagnation

The reversed *Knight of Cups* encourages you to turn emotional challenges into opportunities for growth and self-discovery. Even in moments of emotional turbulence, there is a wonderful opportunity to learn and evolve. Instead of being swayed by negative emotions, use them as a mirror to understand your deeper fears and desires. Confront your insecurities head-on, recognising them as indicators of areas where you need to grow. These emotions are your soul calling out to you, asking you to embrace the lessons they bring and use them for healing. By doing so, you discover reliability, stability, and empowerment, moving past stagnation and evolving into your highest potential.

Reflection

In what way can I address my insecurities and transform them into opportunities for personal growth and resilience?

How can I balance my idealistic dreams with realistic actions to move beyond stagnation and unreliability?

Queen of Cups

Your heart guides you towards balanced, spiritual fulfilment.

Empathy, compassion, intuition, emotional balance, deep understanding, nurturing

The *Queen of Cups* signifies nurturing yourself and others, the presence of children, or a newly birthed, young-at-heart creation. Nurture your intuitive gifts and let the gentle guidance of your empathetic heart lead you to a place of emotional balance and deep understanding. By fostering a space for self-care, you heal your soul and create ripples of love and support for those around you. Open to the beauty of unconditional love. Let it radiate through every aspect of your life, empowering you to manifest a world where empathy, compassion, and creativity are celebrated. Trust in the innate wisdom of your heart, for it holds the key to unlocking the boundless potential of your spirit and the harmonious life you desire.

Reflection

How can I cultivate empathy, compassion, and emotional balance within myself to enhance my personal growth and relationships?

In what ways can I nurture my intuition and spiritual wellbeing to deepen my understanding of the world?

seeking your counsel. Trust your innate capacity to remain poised amidst life's challenges, cultivating a sanctuary of balance and growth for yourself and those around you. As you embody the *King of Cups*, your loving presence becomes a beacon of inspiration, guiding others to discover their own path of emotional resilience and spiritual growth.

Reflection

How can I apply the wisdom of the King of Cups *to approach conflicts with empathy, understanding, and emotional intelligence?*

What strategies can I adopt to maintain inner balance and remain calm during difficult conversations or disagreements?

Reversed

Overcome life's obstacles with compassion and understanding.

Manipulation, moodiness, disconnection, instability, impatience, jealousy, intolerance

This card reversed suggests reflecting on and transforming challenging traits within yourself and your interactions with others. Explore the origins of these feelings and understand them as seeds that, when nurtured, blossom into growth and deeper empathy. By embracing this wisdom, you foster emotional stability and reconnect with the depth of your wisdom and patience.
This journey involves sailing gracefully through the turbulent waters of your moods, viewing each experience as a valuable lesson to enrich your emotional intelligence and compassion.
As you navigate these challenges, equip yourself to manage complex, sensitive scenarios more effectively, evolving into a more understanding, tolerant, and emotionally well-rounded individual.

Reflection

What personal traits or behaviours do I need to work on to cultivate a more emotionally stable and compassionate approach to life's challenges?

How can I gain a deeper understanding of my feelings of jealousy, impatience, or moodiness and transform them into positive attributes?

The Suit of Pentacles
Material and Earthly Matters

Step into the **fertile grounds** of the suit of Pentacles, where the earth beneath your feet becomes **a canvas for manifestation**. This suit invites us to explore the tangible aspects of our existence, from financial prosperity to physical wellbeing. By tending to the seeds of abundance with diligence and patience, we cultivate a rich harvest in the garden of our lives. In Soul Mirroring, the suit of Pentacles reflects the external manifestations of our inner beliefs about abundance and prosperity. By observing the state of our material world, we gain insights into the areas of our consciousness that require nurturing to bring about positive transformation.

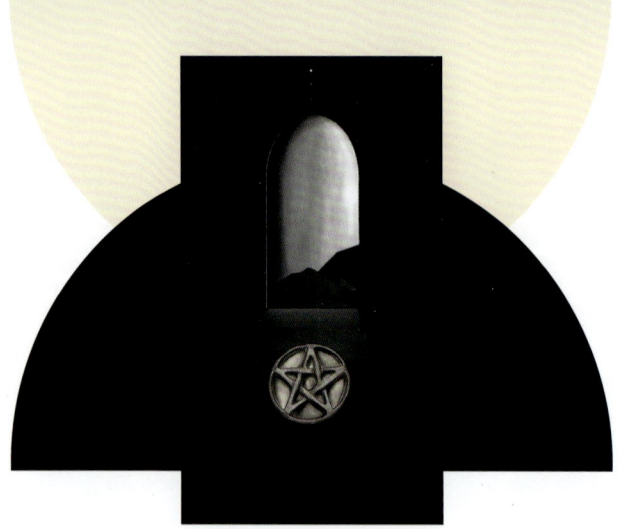

Ace of Pentacles

Seize the golden opportunity before you!

Prosperity, opportunity, manifestation, stability, growth, abundance, reward

The *Ace of Pentacles* signifies the merging of opportunity and prosperity, a moment when the seeds of abundance beckon to be sown and the fruits of your labours picked. Surrender to the cosmic gifts presenting themselves and allow your aspirations to anchor themselves firmly in the fertile soil of your life. Have faith in your capabilities and gifts, as they will serve as the compass guiding you through this transformative journey of growth and realisation. As you tend to your ambitions with care, witness them blossom into a reality that surpasses your desires, bestowing upon you the rewards and fulfilment that you truly deserve.

Reflection

What opportunities for growth and abundance are currently present in my life that I can nurture and develop further?

How can I use my unique skills and talents to manifest my desired prosperity and success?

Reversed

Unlock your hidden potential and rise above the challenges.

Missed opportunity, financial loss, stagnation, instability, greed, lack, insecurity

The reversed *Ace of Pentacles*—reflecting stagnation, instability, and insecurity—invites you to delve into your personal strengths and weaknesses. Embrace lessons of missed opportunities and financial challenges as avenues to unlocking your hidden potential. Reassess your path and recognise every setback as a stepping stone towards greater wisdom and self-awareness. Confront your fears and insecurities head-on, understanding they merely reflect internal knots needing to be untangled. This is a period for introspection and recalibration, where a perceived sense of lack or greed transforms into a powerful motivation for change. By acknowledging and addressing these challenges, you learn vital lessons about resilience, adaptability, and the true value of resources, both material and spiritual. Let this phase be a catalyst for reinvention and realignment with your true values and goals, guiding you back to a path of abundance and stability.

Reflection

What recent setbacks or challenges can I reframe as opportunities for personal growth and development?

In what ways can I transform my fears and perceived lacks into motivations for positive change and abundance in my life?

Two of Pentacles

Balance life with elegance and harmony amidst the ever-shifting tides.

Balance, adaptability, flexibility, juggling, change, resourcefulness, duality

The *Two of Pentacles* calls for graceful balance and adaptability as you navigate life's constant flux. Embrace the dynamic dance of change by moving with the natural rhythms around you, guided by poise and inner steadiness. Practice the art of adaptability, prioritise your goals with intention, and harness the power of resilience and resourcefulness. In this fluid journey, find harmony amidst the chaos and allow yourself to be attuned to the subtle rhythms of the Universe, knowing these shifts happen for good reason. By navigating these transformative tides with unwavering focus and a willingness to learn, you grow stronger, wiser, and capable of manifesting a bountiful life.

Reflection

How can I improve my ability to maintain balance when faced with life's challenges and changes?

How can I recognise and embrace the opportunities for growth and learning that present themselves during times of change and uncertainty?

What strategies can I implement to prioritise my time and energy better, ensuring I focus on what truly matters?

Reversed

Transform chaos into clarity by embracing flexibility.

Imbalance, burnout, overwhelm, disorganisation, inflexibility, stress

In the reversed position, the *Two of Pentacles* urges you to find serenity in the midst of chaos and transform imbalance into a path towards clarity. It reflects the challenges of burnout, serving as a mirror to recognise and address areas in your life that are out of sync. Re-evaluate your priorities, embrace flexibility, and let go of the need to control every aspect of your life. This period of turmoil is not just a test of your resilience but an opportunity to develop a deeper understanding of your needs and boundaries. By adapting to these challenges with self-compassion and a willingness to shift your approach, you find a new equilibrium aligning more authentically with your true self, leading to a peaceful, balanced, and fulfilling life.

Reflection

Where in my life am I experiencing imbalance, and how can I approach these areas with flexibility and openness?

What lessons can I learn from feelings of overwhelm and burnout to create a more harmonious and sustainable lifestyle?

How can I use this period of stress as an opportunity to redefine my priorities and align more closely with my true values and desires?

Three of Pentacles

Collaborate and create a powerful pathway to success.

Cooperation, collaboration, teamwork, skill, expertise, commitment

The *Three of Pentacles* invites you into the enriching realm of collaboration, where the harmonious union of diverse skills and perspectives fosters an environment ripe for growth and achievement. Embrace the power of teamwork and allow the unique talents of everyone to shine as you work together towards a shared vision. Through open communication, commitment, and mutual respect, create a foundation that supports the manifestation of your collective aspirations. As you weave the threads of your united goals, you elevate your individual accomplishments and contribute to raising the collective consciousness, propelling humanity towards a more harmonious future.

Reflection

How can I better communicate and listen to the ideas and perspectives of others to create a more harmonious and productive team dynamic?

What steps can I take to ensure that I am contributing to a shared vision for success while still honouring my unique strengths and talents?

Reversed

Foster open communication and understanding to create a shared vision.

Isolation, noncooperation, miscommunication, conflict, competition, disagreements

This card in reverse reflects the internal barriers or fears hindering your ability to engage in cooperative endeavours. Examine and address feelings of competition or disagreement, urging you to find common ground and shared goals. Develop deeper empathy, listen actively, and express your thoughts clearly. In doing so, you create a pathway towards building stronger, more unified team dynamics. Value differences and work through conflicts with compassion and patience. Open yourself up to new ideas, perspectives, and successful partnerships. When collaboration seems one-sided, it's a sign to reassess your approach. This awareness nurtures your personal growth and empowers you to make informed decisions aligned with your values, leading to more fulfilling and effective partnerships.

Reflection

In what ways can I actively seek to understand and bridge gaps in communication with those around me?

What personal fears or barriers might affect my ability to collaborate effectively, and how can I work through these to foster a more harmonious working relationship?

Four of Pentacles

Cultivate a strong foundation of internal self-security.

Possessiveness, security, control, investment, conservation, prudence, savings

The *Four of Pentacles* invites you to examine your relationship with material possessions and cultivate a balanced approach towards security and abundance. While it is important to establish a foundation of stability and control, be mindful of not becoming overly possessive or clinging to the material things in your life. True security comes from within — your worth is not determined by possessions external to you. As you let go of your attachment to things, create space for the generosity of the Universe to flow into your life. Trust in the power of letting go and embrace the freedom that comes from vulnerability and openness. By doing so, you open yourself to unexpected opportunities and fulfilment.

Reflection

What steps can I take to establish a sense of inner worth and security that is independent of my external circumstances or possessions?

How can I cultivate a healthy balance between my desire for stability and security and my willingness to remain open to the abundance of the Universe?

In what ways can I let go of attachments to material possessions and embrace a more open approach to life?

Reversed

Trust that the Universe will provide in unexpected ways.

Generosity, release, openness, vulnerability, freedom, spontaneity, flexibility

This reversed card signifies introspection and release, so reflect on your relationship with material possessions and the deeper fears tied to them. Shift from clinging to material security to embracing the liberating currents of generosity, openness, and flexibility. True wealth is found in the richness of experiences, emotional connections, and personal growth. Letting go of rigid attachments allows you to flow with life's changes, opening up to spontaneous joys and unexpected opportunities. Value the fleeting and intangible aspects of life, understanding that generosity of spirit often leads to abundance in unexpected forms. Embracing vulnerability and releasing the need for stringent security paves the way for a more flexible, open-hearted existence where you can experience true freedom and swim in the wellspring found within.

Reflection

How can embracing vulnerability and releasing my grip on material security enrich my life?

What fears or beliefs about material possessions am I holding on to, and how can I release them to welcome abundance in all its forms?

In what ways can practising generosity and openness lead to unexpected opportunities and personal growth?

Five of Pentacles

You have the strength to emerge from the darkness into the light.

Hardship, material loss, poverty, illness, abandonment, struggle, scarcity

The *Five of Pentacles* signifies times of struggle and loss but also holds the promise of resilience and recovery. Because even in the darkest of times, you are enveloped in a loving embrace that guides you towards the light. These moments of struggle and hardship are not meant to break you but to illuminate a path towards growth and healing. Believe in the mirror the Universe reflects, knowing each challenge is an opportunity to tap into your strength and wisdom. As you navigate these difficult times with truth, discover new insights and perspectives that help you move towards a future more aligned with your truth. Embrace the power of transformation and renewal and be guided by the loving presence surrounding you. Realise that the timing of events in your life aligns with your internal readiness, not external circumstances. Everything is happening as it is, and the Universe (i.e., you, your true being) guides you towards the right path at the right time.

Reflection

How can I shift my perspective to view the challenges and struggles in my life as opportunities for growth and transformation?

How can I cultivate a mindset of abundance and gratitude, even when faced with scarcity and lack?

What practices can I adopt to help me remain centred and grounded and remind myself of the loving presence that surrounds me?

Reversed

Adopt a new perspective to illuminate the path.

Hope, acceptance, renewal, gratitude, positivity, healing, contentment

This card speaks to a turning point, where you begin to find a renewed sense of hope and healing despite external hardships. While challenges such as material loss, abandonment, or scarcity may be beyond your control, the way you respond can shape your journey forward. Rather than blaming yourself for these difficulties, this reversal invites you to focus on your resilience and the inner strength that has carried you through. It's a reminder that even in tough times, there are small victories to celebrate and moments of gratitude that can lift your spirit. This phase of renewal helps you to shift your mindset towards one of acceptance and growth, empowering you to move beyond the hardship with newfound clarity and strength. By embracing this perspective, you open the door to healing and the possibility of a brighter, more contented future.

Reflection

How can I honour my resilience and inner strength during times of difficulty?

What practices can help me cultivate hope and healing, even when life feels overwhelming?

Six of Pentacles

The cycle of support creates abundance for all.

Generosity, charity, giving, sharing, assistance, philanthropy, balance

The *Six of Pentacles* urges you to give generously in order to create abundance and balance in your life. By extending a helping hand to those in need, you are setting in motion a cycle of support and abundance that uplifts you also. True prosperity comes from giving freely and sharing your blessings with others, not from holding material possessions tight. Trust in the power of balance and fairness — when you give from your heart, you also receive spiritual, emotional, and physical abundance in return. Embrace the interconnectedness of all things and recognise the abundance within and around you. Thus, you create a more fulfilling and purposeful life guided by love and compassion.

Reflection

How can I cultivate a greater sense of generosity and compassion towards myself and others to create a more fulfilling and meaningful life?

What aspects of my life can I share with others to create a cycle of support and abundance that benefits us all?

Reversed

Break free from imbalance and embrace the power of generosity and fairness.

Greed, selfishness, exploitation, inequality, unfairness, dependence, scarcity

The *Six of Pentacles* in reverse reflects an internal imbalance between giving and receiving, emphasising the need to establish a more equitable distribution of resources and support. By acknowledging and addressing your own tendencies towards hoarding or dependence, you open a pathway to greater generosity and abundance, benefitting not just yourself but those around you as well. This transformation extends beyond financial or material wealth and includes emotional and spiritual generosity. Cultivate a mindset where you perceive abundance in giving and sharing, transforming scarcity into a harmonious, open environment. In doing so, you align yourself with the principles of balance and fairness, fostering a life that is rich in holistic abundance and fulfilment.

Reflection

In what way can I challenge my own attitudes towards greed or selfishness to foster a more generous and giving spirit?

What steps can I take to move away from a mindset of scarcity and towards one of abundance, both in the material and spiritual aspects of my life?

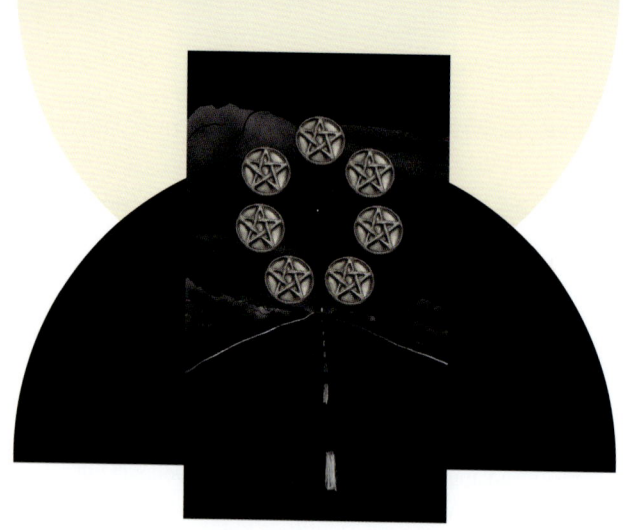

Seven of Pentacles

Your hard work and perseverance will bear bountiful fruit in due time.

Perseverance, patience, investment, hard work, harvest, reward

The *Seven of Pentacles* signifies a time of assessment, evaluation, and patience as you await the fruition of your hard work and dedication. It reminds you that growth and success do not come overnight but are the result of consistent effort and perseverance. As you journey towards your aspirations, have faith in your abilities and maintain a positive outlook. Your efforts will bear fruit in due time; abundance and success will come because of your hard work. Potential setbacks are opportunities for growth and learning rather than roadblocks. Stay focused on your goals and be willing to adjust your strategy as needed. You have the power to manifest the abundance and success you seek by staying positively committed to your path and remaining open to the possibilities you face.

Reflection

What progress have I made towards my goals and aspirations, and what steps can I take to continue moving forward with patience and perseverance?

What lessons can I learn from past setbacks or failures, and how can I apply these lessons to my current efforts towards growth and success?

Reversed

Release impatience and trust in the process of growth.

Impatience, impulsiveness, disappointment, shortcuts, procrastination, unwise investment

This card in reverse reminds you to be wary of impulsive shortcuts and unwise investments that stem from a desire for immediate results. It reflects the necessity to reassess your approach, acknowledging that true progress often requires patience and a steadfast commitment to your long-term vision. Embrace this time as an opportunity to refine your strategies and realign with honest objectives. By understanding that disappointment and procrastination are often signals of misalignment, you can make more informed choices and cultivate a mindset that values the journey as much as the destination. This card encourages you to pause, reflect, and embrace the strength and wisdom that emerges from practising patience.

Reflection

How can I cultivate patience and trust in the timing of my life's journey, especially when facing delays or obstacles?

What impulsive behaviours or shortcuts have I been tempted by, and how can I realign with a more thoughtful and strategic approach?

Eight of Pentacles

Hone your skills with diligence and create a path to success.

Diligence, skill, craftsmanship, hard work, mastery, precision, detail-oriented

The *Eight of Pentacles* represents the power of diligence and dedication to one's craft or skill. Through hard work and a commitment to mastering your craft, you achieve great success and reach your highest potential. The key to achieving mastery lies in staying focused, setting goals, and striving towards improvement every day. Through learning and growth, let the challenges you encounter inspire you to push yourself further. The path to success is not always linear, and setbacks and moments of stagnation are opportunities for reflection and redirection. Trust in your ability to learn and improve, and stay dedicated to your path with unwavering focus and patience. Through your hard work and commitment, you have the power to achieve mastery and create a fulfilling and successful life.

Reflection

What skills or interests ignite my passion, and how can I prioritise dedicating more time to cultivate and master them?

Are there any obstacles or challenges I have encountered on my journey, and can I use them as opportunities for growth and learning?

Reversed

Refocus your energy with patience and precision for success.

Mediocrity, impatience, procrastination, boredom, stagnation, carelessness

This card in reverse signifies the feelings of inferiority and lethargy that have overtaken you while you work towards a goal. A recalibration of your attention is required so you can achieve what you aspire to. This shift signifies a crucial moment for introspection and realignment with your goals. It suggests a need to break free from routines that no longer serve you. Rekindle your passion for learning and improvement. Embrace this opportunity to re-evaluate your approach to your work or craft, identifying areas where you may have been cutting corners or losing focus. In this case, shake up your process a little or try an alternative method to reopen your focus. The reversed *Eight of Pentacles* also inspires you to reignite your commitment to excellence, paying attention to the details that lead to mastery and success. By adopting a more mindful and dedicated approach, you transform periods of stagnation into growth and success.

Reflection

In what areas of my life or work have I been settling for mediocrity, and what actions can I take to elevate my standards and dedication?

How can I reorganise my daily routine to reignite my passion for learning and improvement?

— Nine of Pentacles —

Enjoy the fruits of your labour and revel in abundance.

Prosperity, abundance, luxury, independence, gratitude, wealth, comfort, success

The *Nine of Pentacles* signifies a time of abundance and prosperity. Recognise and celebrate the results of your efforts, and feel proud of your accomplishments. True abundance is not just about material possessions — it's about cultivating a rich inner world that speaks to your truth. Connect with yourself and nurture your spiritual and emotional needs. Release any unhealthy attachments to material things and know that the Universe reflects what is truly you. Allow yourself to bask in the richness and abundance of life, knowing deep down you are worthy of all the blessings coming your way.

Reflection

How can I fully embrace and appreciate the abundance and blessings in my life?

In what ways can I cultivate a deeper sense of self-worth and deservingness?

How can I honour and celebrate my own achievements and accomplishments?

Reversed

Reconnect with your inner abundance and let go of materialism.

Dependence, isolation, materialism, loss, financial struggles, jealousy

In its reversed aspect, the *Nine of Pentacles* gently nudges you towards rediscovering the wealth within your heart and soul. This may be a time when external successes and material gains feel less fulfilling, urging you to turn inwards and cherish the non-material joys of life. Embrace this as an opportunity to cultivate a deeper understanding of your true needs and desires beyond the confines of physical wealth. This phase is not about loss — it's about recognising the abundance that arises from loving relationships, inner peace, and personal growth. Let this be a time of healing, where you lovingly detach from materialism and foster a sense of gratitude for the simple yet profound blessings in life.

Reflection

How can I lovingly embrace the abundance that exists in my life beyond material possessions?

How can I foster inner peace and contentment in my day-to-day experiences?

How can I lovingly let go of external dependencies to strengthen my sense of self and independence?

Ten of Pentacles

Bask in the richness of your abundant blessings.

Legacy, abundance, family, inheritance, prosperity, security, completion, home

The *Ten of Pentacles* represents the moments you are surrounded by the rich tapestry of your ancestors' legacies woven into the very fabric of your being. As you honour their gifts and struggles, you strengthen your connection to our collective evolution. You possess the resilience, wisdom, and blessings of those who came before you. Embrace this history with gratitude and allow it to guide you towards a brighter future. As well as financial maturity, this card signifies inheritance, generosity, or marriage. Trust your innate abilities and the loving support of your close relations, both past and present, as you gracefully move forward with pride and purpose.

Reflection

In what ways do I honour, learn from, and carry on the legacies of my ancestors in my life?

How can I create a sense of generational wealth and abundance for myself and my loved ones in a way that aligns with my values?

Reversed

Times of scarcity remind us to focus on inner wealth.

Loss, scarcity, financial instability, family conflict, disconnection, neglect

When this card is reversed, it suggests the need to reflect on inner wealth during times of external scarcity or family challenges. Such a phase often brings financial instability, loss, or disconnection to light, prompting you to discover strength and abundance within. Redefine prosperity, recognising it not solely in financial terms but also in the wealth of your relationships, experiences, and personal development. Heal family conflicts and reconnect with your roots in a meaningful way. Use this opportunity to see how external challenges reflect internal areas needing growth and attention. Remember, the legacy of your ancestors encompasses more than material wealth — it includes resilience, love, and wisdom. These inner qualities, rich in character, manifest themselves in the physical world, contributing to a sense of abundance. Understand that the light shining from within you is what truly enriches your world.

Reflection

How can I cultivate a sense of abundance and fulfilment that transcends material wealth?

What lessons can I learn from my current challenges that will contribute to my personal growth and the wellbeing of my loved ones?

Page of Pentacles

Embrace opportunities and manifest dreams through dedication.

Opportunity, manifestation, ambition, stability, focus, an offer, potential, diligence

The *Page of Pentacles* signifies a time to seize new opportunities, dedicate yourself to growth, and foster a steadfast commitment to your goals. You are the architect of your destiny. By cultivating patience, discipline, and focus, you harness your inner power and manifest your dreams and aspirations. There is more within you, patiently waiting to be released. Be resourceful and open to learning new skills, and you will find yourself on a path of prosperity and personal success. Trust in your innate potential to create a life of abundance and fulfilment.

Reflection

Can I identify and act upon opportunities that align with my passions and purpose?

How can I embrace a growth mindset to overcome challenges and foster personal development?

In what creative ways can I employ my existing resources to build a foundation for success and abundance?

Reversed

Regain focus and transform potential into achievements.

Procrastination, laziness, insecurity, impatience, distraction, irresponsibility

The period represented by the reversed *Page of Pentacles* is characterised by procrastination, insecurity, or impatience — significant signposts pointing towards deeper internal issues that need attention. Reflect on how external manifestations could be linked to internal blocks such as self-doubt, distraction, or a lack of clear vision. These challenges are opportunities for profound personal growth and transformation. Thus, this card in reverse invites you to rekindle your commitment to your ambitions, embrace a mindset of responsibility, and approach your aspirations with a renewed sense of clarity and determination. Break free from unproductive patterns and nurture your innate capabilities, allowing your latent potential to blossom into tangible achievements. Your path to success is paved with patience, perseverance, and a deep understanding of your inner world, as much as it is with external efforts.

Reflection

How can I identify and dismantle the inner barriers that lead to procrastination, and align my actions more closely with my goals?

In what ways can I compassionately address my insecurities and fears, transforming them into empowering strengths that drive me forward?

Knight of Pentacles

Stay steadfast and cultivate patience for success.

Reliability, steadfastness, dedication, responsibility, patience, perseverance

The *Knight of Pentacles* asks you to harness your steadfast nature and unwavering focus to tackle challenges with grace and determination. Understand the value of hard work and the importance of consistency in achieving your goals. Embrace practical solutions and maintain a strong sense of responsibility towards your commitments. Your perseverance and loyalty guide you towards a path of stability and abundance. As you stay true to your convictions, the Universe will reward your efforts with prosperity and personal growth.

Reflection

How can I foster a strong sense of responsibility and commitment to my goals and relationships?

In what ways can I incorporate practicality and efficiency into my daily routine for better time management?

How can I demonstrate reliability and dedication in my personal and professional life?

Reversed

Break free from stagnation and try something new to spark progression.

Stagnation, rigidity, laziness, boredom, neglect, shortcuts, gambler

Reversed, this card signifies feelings of rigidity, boredom, or a tendency to take shortcuts, signalling a need for a fresh perspective and innovative approaches. Break free from the comfort of routine and the constraints of conventional methods, and challenge yourself to explore new avenues for growth. External signs of stagnation often reflect internal resistance to change or a fear of the unknown. Embrace this as an opportunity to re-evaluate your path, inject creativity and flexibility into your endeavours, and recognise that taking calculated risks can lead to significant advancements. Progress requires a balance between steadfast commitment and a willingness to adapt and evolve. As you navigate this phase, remember that every moment of hesitation or reluctance is an invitation to rekindle your inner fire and drive towards success in a more dynamic and fulfilling path.

Reflection

In what areas of my life could I benefit from introducing new ideas or methods, and how can I implement them?

What steps can I take to strike a balance between maintaining a steady course and being open to innovative approaches for growth?

Queen of Pentacles

Nurture self and others, cultivating abundance through practicality.

Generous, nurturing, practical, comfort, abundance, resourcefulness, prosperity

The *Queen of Pentacles* encourages you to tap into your nurturing and resourceful essence, channelling your inner multitasker. As a symbol of stability and abundance, harness your innate ability to create a sanctuary of comfort and security for you and those you cherish. Your practical and generous nature enables you to cultivate prosperity and harmony in every facet of your existence. Believe in your capacity to care for others while simultaneously achieving your personal goals and nurturing your wellbeing.

By embodying warmth, compassion, and a grounded mindset, you cultivate a life of genuine fulfilment.

Reflection

How can I establish a comforting and secure atmosphere for my loved ones and myself, fostering stability in my environment?

What tangible steps can I implement to promote prosperity and abundance in various aspects of my life?

How can I effectively maintain an equilibrium between my career, family life, and personal wellbeing in a way that promotes long-term health and happiness?

Reversed

Reclaim control and find a balance to overcome obstacles and setbacks.

Defeat, lack of control, imbalance, indecision, delays, aggression, setbacks

When the *Queen of Pentacles* is reversed, it beckons deep introspection into the underlying causes of current hurdles, often mirroring internal discord or a detachment from your fundamental values. It's a pivotal moment to re-evaluate how you care for yourself and others, addressing any inclinations towards unnecessary aggression or overburdening yourself. By acknowledging and working through these issues, you align more closely with your inherent traits of practical wisdom, generosity, and resourcefulness. Setbacks are temporary and serve as catalysts for personal growth and fortitude. Harness your innate resilience, confidently recognising your ability to weather challenging times. As you navigate these obstacles, emerge rejuvenated and poised with the grace of a queen, equipped with a clear and focused vision for the journey ahead.

Reflection

How can I identify and address the internal imbalances that manifest as external challenges in my life?

How can I realign my actions with my core values and priorities to create a more balanced and harmonious life?

King of Pentacles

Achieve prosperity through discipline and leadership.

Security, discipline, leadership, abundance, provider, dependable, practical, prosperous

The *King of Pentacles* invites you to practise the qualities of strength, discipline, and leadership In your pursuit of success and abundance. Recognise the power you possess to create a secure and fulfilling life, symbolised by the King's stability and prosperity. By practising patience and remaining grounded, you inspire others and build a foundation for personal and professional growth. Nurture your connections and emotional wellbeing. Focusing on your ambitions leads to manifesting your dreams and cultivating a life of wealth and contentment through determination and wise guidance. Embrace the responsibility that comes with leadership and use your power to uplift others and make a positive impact on the world.

Reflection

How can I balance my ambitions with nurturing my relationships and emotional wellbeing?

What steps can I take to cultivate patience and dependability in my actions and decision-making?

How can I use my strengths to inspire and guide others on their path to success and abundance?

Reversed

Foster a balance between material and spiritual growth.

Greed, materialism, inflexibility, short-sightedness, irresponsibility, dependence

This card in reverse suggests an imbalance between your focus on material success and the nourishment of your spiritual and emotional wellbeing. Reassess your priorities with love and insight, ensuring your pursuit of material success is balanced with enriching your spiritual and emotional wellbeing. Reflect deeply on how external manifestations might signal an inner imbalance or a disconnection from your authentic self and core values. Drawing this card encourages you to be flexible and open in your thoughts and decisions, avoiding short-term choices for lasting fulfilment. Strive for harmony in your life's journey, crafting a path to prosperity that's responsible, sustainable, and soul-nourishing. True leadership is about more than achieving success — it's about being a beacon of balance, demonstrating the graceful integration of material accomplishments with spiritual depth and ethical principles. This is a golden opportunity for profound personal growth, leading to a life that's successful, deeply fulfilling, and harmoniously balanced.

Reflection

In what ways can I realign my daily actions and decisions with my deeper values and spiritual beliefs, ensuring a more balanced approach to success?

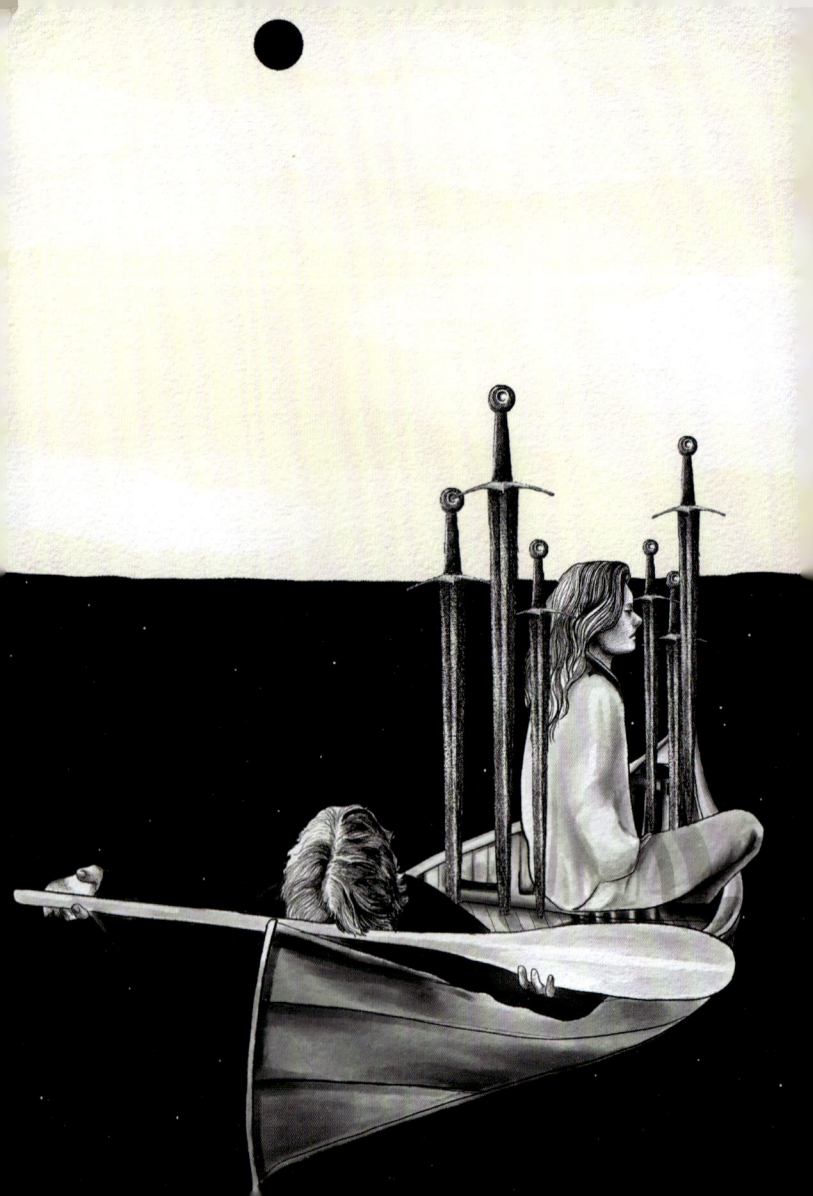

The Suit of Swords
Intellect and Clarity

Journey through the **realm of the intellect**, where the keen blade of discernment cuts through the fog of confusion. The suit of Swords invites us to **explore the landscape of our thoughts and ideas**, cultivating mental clarity and embracing the power of our intellect. As we navigate the intricate dance of logic and reason, we gain the tools to face challenges head-on and make informed decisions on our soul's path. The suit of Swords mirrors the reflective nature of the mind, urging us to examine our thoughts and beliefs with a discerning eye. By honing our mental acuity, we not only enhance our understanding of ourselves but also contribute to the collective consciousness, fostering a deeper connection with the world around us.

Ace of Swords

Trust your intellect and insight to forge your path to success.

Clarity, truth, breakthrough, insight, focus, victory, intellect, decision

The *Ace of Swords* encourages you to harness the power of clarity and insight to navigate your journey with precision and confidence. Tap into your inner wisdom, cut through the fog of uncertainty and trust your intellect. Embrace the transformative power of truth and clarity in your life, and you will find that new doors will open and opportunities will present themselves. It is time to make clear and decisive choices, drawing upon your innate understanding of what is right and just. In doing so, you will find not only victory over obstacles but also a deeper sense of purpose and personal empowerment.

Reflection

What obstacles am I facing, and how can I harness the power of truth and communication to overcome them?

What areas of my life could benefit from increased clarity and focus? How can I better trust my own intellect and intuition in making decisions?

Reversed

Realign your thoughts and act with wisdom.

Confusion, miscommunication, chaos, indecision, illusion, delays, dishonesty

The reversed *Ace of Swords* indicates a period of mental fog, confusion, or indecision, where clarity may feel out of reach. Turn your attention to the currents of your inner world, where thoughts may be swirling in confusion or tangled in webs of miscommunication. It's okay to feel overwhelmed or indecisive at times. It signals a time to pause, breathe, and realign your thoughts with the wisdom of your higher self. Clear the mental fog and confront any illusions. Ask yourself where you might be avoiding uncomfortable truths or self-deceiving. This introspective journey is a powerful step towards self-honesty and clarity, and it is vital for your personal development. It allows you to shed layers that no longer serve you and to emerge with a renewed sense of purpose and understanding. As you navigate through this period, do so with kindness and compassion for yourself. Acknowledge your efforts and progress, no matter how small they may seem. The journey towards intellectual empowerment and clear communication is ongoing and ever-evolving.

Reflection

In what situations have I noticed myself avoiding the truth or being less than honest with myself or others, and how can I approach these situations with integrity and self-compassion?

Two of Swords

Delve deep within to confidently navigate life's crossroads.

Indecision, stalemate, crossroads, avoidance, choices, standstill, tension

The *Two of Swords* encourages you to explore the depths of your inner truth, wisdom, and intuition when facing difficult decisions or confrontations. In the midst of uncertainty, take a moment to pause and reflect on the choices before you. Seek a balance between logic and intuition, acknowledging that the best decisions often come from a harmonious blend of both heart and mind. By going inward, you can find the clarity needed to navigate life's crossroads with confidence and grace. Remember, the power to overcome challenges lies within you, and harnessing this inner strength will lead you to profound personal growth and transformation.

Reflection

In which areas of my life can I benefit from pausing, reflecting, and seeking inner guidance to make more informed choices?

How can I cultivate a deeper connection with my intuition to navigate life's challenges more effectively?

Reversed

Trust your intuition as it guides you towards the right resolution.

Decisions, resolution, compromise, action, clarity, movement, insight, confrontation

The reversed *Two of Swords* indicates you are at the threshold of moving beyond the delicate balance of indecision and standstill in your situation. Like a lighthouse guiding ships through the night, your intuition shines guidance as you approach resolution. Embrace the wisdom within and allow it to illuminate your path through the fog of uncertainty. Believe in your innate ability to make decisions resonant with your core self. It's an opportunity to advance with clarity and insight, transforming the tension you've been feeling into a catalyst for growth and movement. Approach what lies ahead with a heart brimming with courage and a mind clear with understanding. Your journey is beautifully unfolding, guiding you closer to the realisation of your true path and purpose.

Reflection

How can I engage more actively with my intuition, allowing it to guide my decision-making process?

What practical steps can I implement to transition from hesitation to confident action?

How can I channel the tension I'm experiencing into positive momentum, fostering growth and bringing clarity to my path?

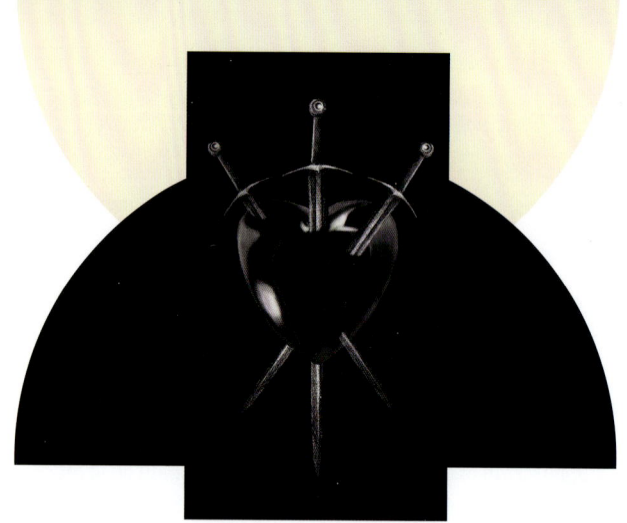

Three of Swords

Acknowledge the pain and allow it to guide you towards healing.

Heartache, sorrow, loss, grief, betrayal, separation, trauma, healing

This card reminds you that your experiences of heartache, sorrow, and loss are opportunities for profound growth and transformation. While it can be challenging to feel the full spectrum of emotions from these experiences, doing so is the first step towards deep healing. By acknowledging your pain, you create space for acceptance, forgiveness, and release. As you move through the healing process, you gain a deeper understanding of yourself and the world around you. By forgiving yourself and others and finding compassion within your heart, you embrace a newfound sense of peace, freedom, and love that is even deeper. Open your heart to the power of healing and emerge stronger, more whole, and more loving than ever before.

Reflection

How can I create a safe space to acknowledge and process my feelings of heartache and loss, allowing for deep healing and growth?

Can I find a balance between honouring my emotions and actively working towards healing and releasing past pain, allowing me to move forward with greater clarity and purpose?

Reversed

Cultivate forgiveness and behold its transformative power for growth and healing.

Forgiveness, healing, recovery, reconciliation, acceptance, learning, release

This card gently nudges you to recognise and release the grievances and hurts that weigh on your heart. Embark on a path of recovery and reconciliation, starting with the most important relationship of all — the one with yourself. Embrace acceptance, not just of the circumstances or actions of others, but of your own vulnerabilities and strengths. This process of forgiveness is not a sign of weakness but a profound act of courage. It allows you to let go of past pains and embrace a future filled with possibility and hope. As you learn to release these emotional burdens, you open doors to new understandings and deeper connections, both within yourself and with others. The journey may be challenging, but it promises a reward of unparalleled growth, peace, and newfound vitality.

Reflection

How can I begin the process of forgiving myself and others, and what steps can I take to engage in this healing practice actively?

How can accepting past hurts aid in my emotional recovery and personal growth?

What lessons have my experiences of hurt and forgiveness taught me, and how can I apply these insights to foster a more loving and compassionate future?

Four of Swords

Take time for rest, reflection, and healing to renew your spirit.

Retreat, rest, contemplation, solitude, healing, recharge, recovery, renewal

The *Four of Swords*' message is clear: Alone time is both sacred and essential. When you retreat and allow yourself the space to recharge, you nurture your human vessel and surrender to receive infinite energy from the Universe. Solitude and contemplation give you the opportunity to connect with the deepest parts of your soul, feel the depths of your inner wisdom, and gain clarity on your path. Through self-reflection and letting go in quiet, you release resistance and cultivate a deeper sense of peace and acceptance, opening up to profound healing and renewal. Taking time for rest and retreat is a powerful act of love that allows you to tap into your innermost being, creating your combined reality from a fully charged and loving source. The wellbeing of yourself and the world are interconnected, and by taking care of yourself, you positively impact those around you. Embrace this opportunity to recharge and renew, and let your light shine bright, illuminating the path towards a more loving and joyful world.

Reflection

How can I prioritise self-care and make time for rest and reflection in my daily life?

What self-limiting beliefs or patterns can I release through reflection to cultivate a deeper sense of peace and acceptance?

How can I approach challenges and obstacles in my life with a mindset of surrender, allowing myself the space to recharge?

Reversed

Healed and rejuvenated, ready to step back into the flow of life.

Restlessness, exhaustion, overworked, stress, resistance, agitation, disconnection

The *Four of Swords* reversed is a gentle yet firm reminder of the risks associated with neglecting rest, starkly cautioning against the path that leads to burnout. Establish a harmonious balance between active pursuits and necessary recuperation, ensuring your energy reserves remain replenished. It may also signal your period of rest reaching its culmination, ushering in a time to advance, or it might alert you that you've been bypassing essential relaxation, inviting exhaustion and stress. Acknowledge and honour the equal importance of rest and engagement in your daily life. Pay close attention to your body's subtle cues, attuning to its unique needs for rest and activity. By embracing this, you'll realign with a beautiful, harmonious rhythm that supports your spirit and wellbeing and empowers you to thrive in all facets of your life.

Reflection

How can I balance the need for rest and action in my life to maintain my wellbeing?

What steps can I take to re-engage with my responsibilities and passions in a way that feels nourishing and sustainable?

Are there areas in my life where I might be resisting necessary rest or, conversely, avoiding re-engagement with the world?

Five of Swords

Transform tension into growth and turn defeat into a powerful lesson.

Conflict, tension, defeat, betrayal, loss, dishonour, ego, competition, aggression

During the strife and discord represented by the *Five of Swords*, it is crucial to establish and maintain healthy boundaries while still fostering love and compassion so you don't become overwhelmed by adversity. Defeat or betrayal prompts you to reassess your relationships, ensuring you prioritise your wellbeing and personal growth. Though the path may be difficult, it is through these challenges that you learn to speak your truth and protect your emotional space with love and fairness. There is strength in knowing your limits and asserting your boundaries with respect. As you navigate these trials, be mindful of your own needs and stay true to your values. By doing so, you cultivate an empowered sense of self, paving the way for more harmonious and meaningful connections.

Reflection

How can I transform conflicts or challenges into opportunities for growth and new perspectives?

What lessons have I learned from past experiences that can help me navigate future conflicts more effectively?

In what way can I assert my boundaries while maintaining respect and compassion for others?

Reversed

Healing and growth come with compromise and understanding.

Reconciliation, forgiveness, compromise, resolution, learning, humility, recovery

The reversed *Five of Swords* embodies the journey from conflict and discord towards a place of understanding, compromise, and reconciliation. It's a reminder that true strength lies in recognising the value of peace and resolution, not in winning every battle. Embrace the healing process, let go of past grudges, and open your heart to forgiveness for others and yourself. This reversed card signifies a pivotal moment of self-reflection, where you learn to communicate more effectively, seek mutually beneficial outcomes, and understand the deeper lessons from past conflicts. As you navigate this reflection, you cultivate a more harmonious and balanced approach to life's challenges, empowering yourself with a renewed sense of purpose and a deeper connection to your inner wisdom.

Reflections

In what areas of my life am I holding on to past conflicts or grudges, and how can I begin the process of forgiveness and reconciliation?

How can I approach challenging situations with more humility, understanding, and a willingness to compromise in order to foster healing and growth for all involved?

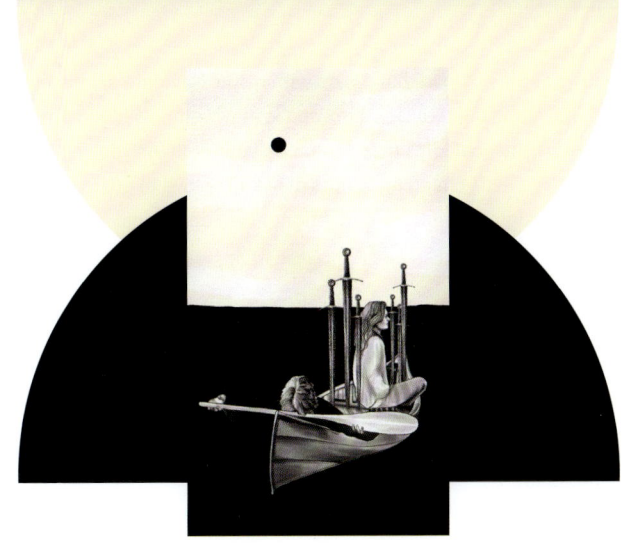

Six of Swords

Navigate transitions with grace and continue on life's journey.

Change, transition, journey, moving on, release, departure, distance

The *Six of Swords* signals a time of transition, encouraging you to leave behind what no longer serves you and move forward towards healing and growth. Release the burdens of past pain, allowing your heart to open and heal as you venture through deep waters with hope and inner strength. The challenges you encounter are opportunities to deepen your understanding and connection to yourself and others. Trust your capacity to adapt and release, for it is within this heartfelt journey that you uncover new horizons and the depths of love that reside within you. Navigate each step with grace and compassion, knowing love will empower you to surmount any obstacles that appear on your path. As you sail through the ever-changing waters of life, may love to guide you towards progress, freedom, and bright new beginnings.

Reflection

What can I learn from my current journey that will empower me to face future obstacles with grace and resilience?

Can I welcome change and transition as opportunities for personal growth and inner healing? What can I release to create space for a lighter heart?

Reversed

Address unresolved issues to move forward with clarity and freedom.

Resistance, delay, stagnation, procrastination, struggle, avoidance, trapped

This reversed card reveals resistance, delay, or stagnation holding you back, suggesting a period of introspection to understand the root of procrastination or avoidance. Address unresolved issues hindering your progress, guiding you to a path of clarity and freedom. Acknowledge and address the struggles or fears trapping you and preventing smooth transitions. Embrace this as an opportunity to delve into your inner self. Uncover and release whatever binds you to the past or impedes your journey forward. Facing these challenges may be daunting, but it's a necessary step to move towards a future filled with greater peace and freedom. By addressing these unresolved issues, you liberate yourself, opening up to wonderful new possibilities and a renewed sense of direction in life.

Reflection

What unresolved issues or fears might be causing stagnation in my life, and how can I confront them to heal?

What steps can I take to transform feelings of being trapped or delayed into positive momentum for my journey?

Seven of Swords

Draw upon your inner resourcefulness and strategic thinking to navigate deception.

Deception, strategy, cunning, secrecy, dishonesty, manipulation, evasion, protect

The *Seven of Swords* encourages you to rely on your wit and inner strength when dealing with situations that involve manipulation. Cultivate a deep sense of self-love and self-respect as you navigate through life's challenges. Protect your emotional boundaries with tenderness and compassion while staying attuned to the energies around you. Resist the urge to resort to dishonest behaviour, and instead, trust your innate wisdom and resourcefulness to navigate through difficult situations. Embrace the transformative power of honesty and accountability, for it is through these values that you build trust and foster soul-aligned, authentic connections with those around you. Even in moments of vulnerability, you face obstacles with grace and integrity, with love as your guiding force and light.

Reflection

What resources or skills can I draw upon to navigate situations involving deception and manipulation with integrity and grace?

How can I better protect my emotional boundaries without compromising my values or authenticity?

What fears or limiting beliefs may be holding me back from embracing honesty and accountability?

Reversed

Rebuild trust by facing consequences with integrity.

Transparency, openness, accountability, confession, guilt, exposure, confrontation

The reversed *Seven of Swords* encourages you to rebuild trust by facing the consequences of your actions with honesty and integrity. Transparency becomes a powerful tool for healing during this time, where owning up to past mistakes, even those wrapped in guilt or discomfort, leads to personal liberation. Confessing your true thoughts and feelings may feel intimidating, but it opens the door to deeper connections and self-awareness. Take this opportunity to confront and resolve any lingering deceptions or misunderstandings. By embracing vulnerability, you demonstrate true strength and authenticity, fostering an atmosphere of honesty and trust in both your relationship with yourself and with others.

Reflection

How can embracing transparency and openness help me rebuild trust in myself and in my relationships?

In what way can I practise accountability and confront my actions to foster healing and understanding?

What steps can I take to transform feelings of guilt or regret into positive actions towards myself and others?

Eight of Swords

Break free from limiting beliefs and soar beyond self-imposed boundaries.

Trapped, isolation, restriction, anxiety, fear, self-doubt, victimhood, paralysis

The upright *Eight of Swords* signifies feeling trapped by your own limiting beliefs, unable to see a way out of the mental or emotional constraints. You are far more powerful than the limitations you've placed on yourself and beyond what your current circumstances may suggest. You are so much more than your perceived limitations, so much more than this physical reality. You possess an inner strength and resilience that breaks you free from the perceived chains that bind you. Shift your focus from what's holding you back to what's possible. Anything is possible if you can imagine it, so trust your power to overcome any obstacles in your way. Release yourself from limiting beliefs and negative self-talk that hold you back, and move forward with clarity, confidence, and love. Embrace your true, exponential inner being and take that first step, knowing you can achieve anything you set your heart on. It's time to release your self-imposed cage and fly.

Reflection

What limiting beliefs and self-talk am I holding on to that are hindering my progress?

Can I shift my focus from what's holding me back to what's possible? How can I reframe my current situation as an opportunity for growth and transformation?

Reversed

Claim your inner strength and step forward into a world of possibilities.

Freedom, release, empowerment, self-awareness, clarity, confidence, courage

The reversed *Eight of Swords* represents a turning point where you begin to break free from self-imposed limitations and reclaim your personal power. Reclaim your inner strength and courage, and step forward into a world brimming with possibilities. This is a moment of empowerment and self-awareness, where you are called to shed the veil of fear and uncertainty that clouds your vision. Embrace the clarity that comes with freedom, and allow it to guide you towards confidence and courage in your decisions. The barriers you face are lessons in disguise, teaching you the resilience and determination needed to take the next step in your personal growth. This change signifies your inner strength, urging you to break free from your mental constraints and step into a world of possibilities.

Reflection

What old beliefs about my abilities and potential am I ready to release and how can this shift in perspective open new opportunities for me?

What is the first step I can take towards embracing this newfound freedom and empowerment?

Nine of Swords

Love resides beyond the boundaries of fear, waiting to be discovered.

Anxiety, fear, nightmares, guilt, despair, loneliness, stress, insomnia

The *Nine of Swords* signifies it's time to release the heavy weight of worry crippling you and trust your ability to overcome the challenges that you face. You possess immense strength and resilience, like a guiding light leading you towards a place of tranquillity. Let go of guilt, self-blame, and judgement, and practise forgiveness towards yourself and others. Take a step towards healing and acceptance, allowing yourself to find clarity and understanding amid chaos. You have the power to transform your fears into love and awaken a deep sense of compassion within yourself. Call upon your innate wisdom and allow divine healing to fill the cavity left by fear, knowing the Universe supports you. Take that first step towards a life of inner peace, and trust in your ability to find your way towards the light.

Reflection

What fears or anxieties am I currently holding on to that are keeping me from finding inner peace?

Can I shift my focus from negative thoughts and emotions to a more positive, compassionate perspective?

How can I reframe my current situation as an opportunity for growth and learning rather than a source of fear and despair?

Reversed

Release the weight of worry and find inner peace and clarity.

Release, relief, acceptance, forgiveness, healing, clarity, inner peace

The *Nine of Swords* reversed signifies a time for profound healing, where acceptance and forgiveness become your allies in overcoming the shadows of anxiety and despair. If you find yourself lying awake at night, consumed by worries about the future, observe these anxieties not as inherent truths but as reflections of internal narratives. These fears are rooted in past experiences or taught beliefs, not in the reality of your present capabilities or worth. Acknowledge your past fears and pains, but allow yourself to let them go, understanding they no longer serve your present or future. Embrace the relief that comes with this release, and find solace in the newfound clarity of your mind and heart. This phase of your life is about nurturing your wellbeing, knowing that true strength comes from vulnerability and the courage to face your inner pain. As you heal, you open the door to a deeper sense of inner peace, one that resonates with the rhythm of your true self.

Reflection

What are the specific worries keeping me awake at night, and what do they reveal about my deeper fears or beliefs?

What steps can I take to cultivate forgiveness and acceptance, both for myself and others, as a path to healing and inner peace?

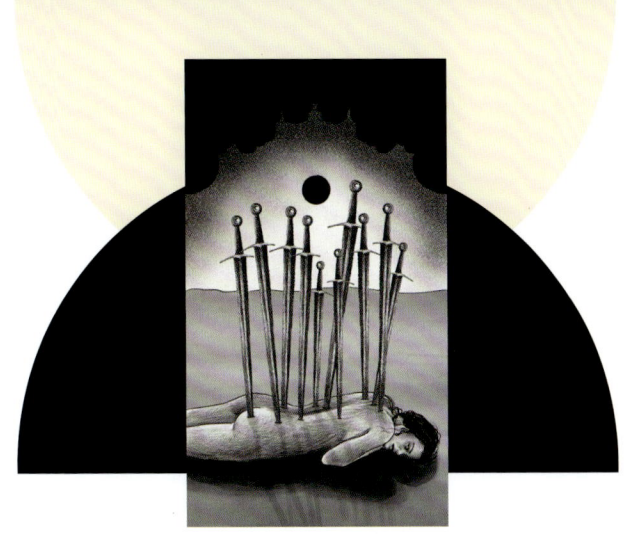

Ten of Swords

*From the depths of pain, emerge stronger
and wiser than before.*

Betrayal, pain, endings, loss, rock bottom, finality, transition

The *Ten of Swords* lovingly guides you to acknowledge the pain and endings in your life, offering you the space to heal and grow stronger through acceptance. Acknowledge the weight of what has happened, and allow yourself to grieve. The betrayal or hurt you've experienced is real, but it also signals that this chapter is closing. Your heart is capable of tremendous healing and transformation. Release the pain you're holding on to, and trust in the power of love and forgiveness to guide you towards a new beginning. Though you may feel lost now, this pain is not the end of your story.

It is a stepping stone towards greater wisdom and growth. You can draw upon your inner strength, knowing you can rise from this moment and move forward into a bright new future.

Reflection

In what ways can I release the weight of past hurts and traumas and move towards forgiveness and healing?

What new beginnings or opportunities may await me, and will I trust in the process of transition and rebirth?

Reversed

*Release the pain of the past and embrace
the power of rebirth.*

Release, hope, recovery, healing, renewal, rebirth, forgiveness

The reversed *Ten of Swords* signals that you are moving beyond the darkest times, ready to release the pain that once weighed heavily on you. This card suggests a turning point where the worst has passed, and healing is now possible. Holding on to past trauma is no longer necessary; it's time to let go of that emotional burden, as it no longer serves your growth. By consciously deciding to release the hurt, you open yourself to forgiveness and the healing that comes with it. Embrace this moment of renewal as a powerful opportunity for rebirth. This is a period of recovery and hope, where you can emerge stronger and more resilient than before. Trust that this process of transformation will lead to wisdom, empowerment, and a renewed sense of self.

Reflection

How can I actively work towards releasing the pain and trauma from my past experiences?

What steps can I take to embrace forgiveness, both towards myself and others, as a path to healing?

In what way can I open myself to the possibilities of renewal in my life?

Page of Swords

Follow your intellectual curiosity and boldly communicate your truth.

Curiosity, intellect, communication, ambition, cleverness, wit, observation

The *Page of Swords* invites you to harness your natural curiosity and sharp intellect as you navigate new experiences and ideas. Allow your curiosity to guide you towards greater understanding, and believe in your intellectual capabilities to navigate through the waves of life. As you explore new ideas and concepts, do so with an open heart and mind and see the divine lessons embedded within each experience. Communicate truth without fear, with a loving, compassionate spirit, honouring the unique perspectives and wisdom of those around you. When you feel restless or indecisive, listen to your inner voice and seek clarity from a place of love and self-awareness. Growth is divinely guided and reflected in your inner being, and each step you take is a step towards your highest good. May your inquisitive nature guide you to a deeper understanding, and may you radiate with the warmth of your inner light.

Reflection

How can I communicate my thoughts and ideas in a way that is constructive and empowering to myself and others?

Can I tap into my inner genius to navigate through challenges and obstacles?

How can I actively listen and remain open-minded to the perspectives and wisdom of others?

Reversed

Take time for introspection and seek clarity before acting impulsively.

Dishonesty, confusion, indecision, inaccuracy, recklessness, cunning, manipulation

The *Page of Swords* reversed signifies a time to pause and reflect amidst moments of confusion and impulsiveness. This mindful approach enables you to gather complete and accurate information, ensuring your actions and words are rooted in truth and consideration. Cherish this period as an opportunity to develop clear, honest, and thoughtful communication. Give yourself the grace to think things through thoroughly, making sure your decisions and expressions align with your deepest values and integrity. This message serves as a loving guide, steering you towards thoughtful actions and heartfelt interactions. Remember to 'sleep on it' when necessary.

Reflection

How can I incorporate patience and reflection in my decision-making process to ensure it aligns with my core values?

How can I improve my communication to be clearer, more honest, and more understanding?

What steps can I take to gracefully address any confusion or misunderstandings in my interactions with others?

Knight of Swords

Use your sharp mind and swift actions to overcome the challenges ahead.

Action, ambition, focus, impulsiveness, restlessness, speed, urgency, intellectual

This card symbolises your remarkable intelligence, powerful actions, and unstoppable determination. Your mind is sharp, your will is strong, and you have everything you need to accomplish anything you set your mind to. However, it's important to balance your passion with love and compassion for yourself and those around you. Take a moment to ground yourself and approach any challenges with thoughtfulness and care. Remember to be kind to yourself and others, and always act with integrity and honesty.

Let the *Knight of Swords* inspire you to lead with courage and confidence and pursue your desires with unwavering commitment. You have the power to achieve greatness, so take graceful action and watch your dreams come to fruition.

Reflection

Can I balance my ambition with love and compassion for myself and others?

How can I stay grounded and avoid impulsive behaviour when faced with challenges?

What opportunities am I being called towards, and how can I move forward with courage and grace?

Reversed

Approach challenges with thoughtfulness and care.

Aggression, impatience, inflexibility, recklessness, stubbornness, turbulence, forceful

The *Knight of Swords* in reverse suggests that impulsiveness and forceful behaviour may be creating unnecessary challenges in your life. Consider the challenges with patience and mindfulness, avoiding the temptation to react with haste or force. This is an opportunity to reflect on your actions and consider the impact of your decisions. For instance, if you find yourself acting hastily or forcefully in a situation, see this behaviour as a reflection of inner turbulence or impatience. Recognise the importance of pausing and reassessing your approach, allowing space for flexibility and understanding. This reversed card gently reminds you that strength lies not only in swift action but also in the wisdom to know when to be still and reflective. Embrace a balanced approach, combining intellectual prowess with emotional intelligence. By doing so, you navigate your path with a harmonious blend of vigour and grace, avoiding the pitfalls of recklessness or stubbornness.

Reflection

In what ways can I practise patience and flexibility to improve my responses to challenging situations?

What strategies can I use to balance my natural drive and ambition with emotional intelligence and empathy?

Queen of Swords

Your inner wisdom will articulate your truth with clarity.

Clarity, communication, intelligence, honesty, wisdom, objectivity, perception, fairness

This card reflects your ability to see things clearly and communicate from a place of wisdom and integrity. Embody the strength of your mind and the power of your voice. You possess an unparalleled ability to perceive the truth and speak it with clarity and precision. Trust your inner wisdom, and let it guide you towards a path aligned with your highest good. Balance your intellect with love and compassion, and approach situations with kindness and empathy. Let your sharp mind and eloquent voice be used for the collective good and inspire and uplift those around you. Stand up for what you believe in and speak your truth with love, confidence, and conviction. Let the spirit of the *Queen of Swords* guide you to fulfil your destiny courageously and compassionately.

Reflection

In what way can I use my intelligence and wisdom to make a positive impact on the world?

How can I balance my intellect with love and compassion in my interactions with others?

In what ways can I inspire and uplift those around me with my words and actions?

Reversed

Open your heart and approach situations with kindness.

Cold, cruel, harsh, inflexible, intolerant, manipulative, secretive, unforgiving

This card in reverse suggests you're being inflexible or intolerant in your interactions. This behaviour mirrors an unacknowledged need for emotional openness and empathy within yourself. Open your heart and approach situations with kindness, moving away from tendencies towards coldness or harshness. Blend your intellectual clarity and perceptiveness with a compassionate heart. Acknowledge the strength in being vulnerable and empathetic, understanding how true wisdom encompasses an open mind and heart. Communicate with honesty, intelligence, warmth, and understanding. In doing so, you transform potential negative traits like cruelty or manipulation into opportunities for healing and connection. Let the reversed *Queen of Swords* be a gentle reminder to infuse your interactions with understanding and forgiveness, nurturing a balance between intellectual insight and emotional wisdom.

Reflection

How can I ensure my communication is clear, honest, kind, and empathetic?

In what ways can I practise being more open and flexible in my interactions with others?

How can I transform my experiences of being harsh or unforgiving into opportunities for personal growth and deeper connections?

King of Swords

Use your intellect and mastery to achieve success and make a difference.

Authority, discipline, fair, honest, intellectual, justice, mastery, powerful, serious

The *King of Swords* signifies a time for clear perception, where your strong leadership skills and ability to make tough decisions with confidence and authority shine through. You have a deep understanding of the world around you and are respected for your wisdom and intellect. But, be mindful of the potential for arrogance and coldness and strive to cultivate compassion and empathy in your interactions with others. By embodying the spirit of this archetype, you inspire positive change and lead others towards a brighter future. Use your mastery of reason and logic to achieve your goals and manifest your highest potential. Trust your inner wisdom and let it guide you towards success and fulfilment.

Reflection

In what way can I use my position to uplift and empower those around me?

How can I balance my intellect with compassion and empathy in my interactions with others?

Can I cultivate a greater sense of interconnectedness while honouring my individuality and independence?

Reversed

Open your mind and heart to different perspectives.

Arrogance, coldness, cruelty, dishonesty, domination, harshness, vindictiveness, selfishness, rigidity, intolerance

The reversed *King of Swords* warns of the potential for becoming too rigid, cold, or domineering in your approach, where intellect overpowers empathy. This card encourages you to blend your intellectual mastery with emotional intelligence. Recognise the strength in being receptive and considerate, understanding how true wisdom and leadership involve listening as much as speaking. Strive to appreciate diverse viewpoints and experiences, knowing how they enrich your understanding of the world. By doing so, you transform negative traits like harshness and rigidity into opportunities for personal growth and inclusive leadership.
Let the reversed *King of Swords* guide your journey towards a balanced approach, where reason is harmonised with compassion and authority is exercised with fairness and kindness.

Reflection

How can I ensure my leadership style is inclusive and respectful of diverse perspectives?

In what way can I practise being more open and flexible in my approach to problem-solving and decision-making?

How can I balance my natural inclination towards logic and authority with a genuine understanding and empathy for others?

The Suit of Wands
Inspiration & Action

Ignite the **flames of inspiration** with the suit of Wands, where creative energy propels us forward on our soul's path. This suit encourages us to **embrace our passions, take bold actions, and pursue our dreams** with unwavering determination. In the practice of Soul Mirroring, the suit of Wands acts as a reflection of our inner fire, mirroring the sparks of enthusiasm and inspiration present in our external pursuits. By aligning our actions with our soul's calling, we not only manifest our desires but also contribute to the collective tapestry of inspiration and evolution of life.

Ace of Wands

Unleash your inner fire and seize new opportunities!

Creativity, inspiration, potential, energy, passion, vitality, new beginnings, growth

The *Ace of Wands* arrives to show how you are an immaculate being of infinite potential, filled with boundless energy and creativity. Tap into this fountain of inspiration and allow it to guide you towards a fulfilling and meaningful life. You are, at your core, a creative being carving out life moment by moment. Be courageous and take the first step towards your dreams, even if it feels uncertain or risky. You have everything you need within you to succeed, so trust that the path unfolding before you is the right one. It may not be easy, but it will be worth it. The world needs your unique gifts and talents, and only you can bring them to life. So go forth with courage and let the flame of your passion light the way. Remember, the Universe is conspiring in your favour. All you need to do is take that first step!

Reflection

How can I align my actions with my true inner desires and values?

What limiting beliefs am I holding on to that are blocking my creative energy and potential?

What is my unique contribution to the world, and how can I use my creativity to bring forth positive change?

Reversed

Release fear and reignite your inner flame.

Blocked creativity, stagnation, indecision, doubt, hesitation, delays, distractions

In its reversed position, the *Ace of Wands* offers an invitation to release fear and rekindle your inner spark, specifically targeting the barriers obstructing your creative power and potential. When you find yourself embedded in hesitation or doubt, recognise how these feelings suppress your creative energy. Reflect on these emotions as mirrors, revealing the internal obstacles that arise from past experiences or self-imposed limits. Embrace this crucial moment as an opportunity to face and let go of these fears, liberating your true creativity and passion. Stagnation and indecision signal a deeper call for introspection and a reconnection with your fundamental desires and values. See this time as a valuable chance to reignite your eagerness for new ventures and growth. By releasing the shackles of doubt and hesitation, you pave the way back to your truth — and in that reflection, achieve your deepest aspirations.

Reflection

What specific fears or doubts are currently hindering my creative expression, and how can I work through them?

In what way can I reconnect with my inner source of inspiration and passion to overcome feelings of stagnation?

Two of Wands

Chart your path and step into limitless possibilities.

Planning, choice, exploration, crossroads, decision, expansion

With the *Two of Wands*, you hold the key to unlocking limitless possibilities in your life. It signifies the time to release limiting beliefs and embrace new opportunities with open arms. Trust the Universe and its infinite abundance, and know that anything you imagine is possible. In order to access these gifts, you must be willing to let go of your fears and take confident, bold action towards your goals. Take ownership of your life and start living with purpose and passion. As you do, the Universe will support you every step of the way, so let go of your doubts and embrace the journey ahead. You have the power within you to achieve greatness and make a positive impact on the world. Take that first step today and start creating the life you've always dreamed of. The world is waiting for you to step into your power and shine your light.

Reflection

How can I use the power of my imagination to create the reality I desire?

Can I expand my horizons and explore new opportunities that align with my passions and values?

What is my vision for my future, and how can I use this to guide my decision-making?

Reversed

Expand your view and trust in the journey ahead.

Indecision, overwhelm, fear of the unknown, limited perspective, controlling

The reversed *Two of Wands* represents indecision, overwhelm, and fear of the unknown. These are times when you are limited by a narrow viewpoint or a desire to maintain control over every aspect of your life. When faced with this, the answer is to embrace a broader perspective and trust the unfolding path. Consider alternative possibilities and pathways, even those that seem unfamiliar or intimidating at first. Trusting your journey means releasing the need for absolute certainty and welcoming the adventure that comes with exploration and openness. This shift in perspective allows for personal growth and learning that a rigid, controlled approach cannot provide. This reversed card nudges you towards flexibility and adaptability because the most fulfilling experiences come from paths that develop naturally. Release your fixed expectations and allow life's journey to lead you to experiences and opportunities resonating with your deepest self coming forth in external expression.

Reflection

Where in my life might I be facing indecision or fear, and how can I adopt a more open and accepting approach to these challenges?

What can I do to ease my need for control and instead trust in life's natural progression and surprises?

Three of Wands

Expand your horizons and embrace new frontiers.

Progress, exploration, anticipation, growth, overseas ventures, milestones, confidence

The *Three of Wands* is your invitation to step out of your comfort zone and embark on a life-changing journey of growth and exploration. Be confident in your ability to lead yourself and others towards your vision for the future. Take bold action, wade new waters, and prepare for what is to come. Keep a positive frame of mind — the path to success is not always linear, so there will be delays and disappointments along the way. However, it is through these challenges that you learn and become stronger. Use these setbacks as an opportunity to realign and gain more clarity on your soul's purpose. You have the power within you to achieve greatness and make a positive impact on the world just by being the most authentic version of yourself. Embrace the journey ahead with confidence and optimism, as every step you take brings you closer to the home of your soul's desire.

Reflection

What opportunities do I currently notice around me? What is my vision for the future, and how can I use this to guide my decision-making?

Can I remain true to myself and stay connected to my innermost values while pursuing my dreams and goals?

Reversed

Use setbacks as an opportunity to realign with your soul's purpose.

Delays, setbacks, frustration, disappointments, poor planning, stagnation

The reversed *Three of Wands* signifies the many factors holding you back from your dreams. These setbacks and delays are not obstacles — they are valuable reflections and opportunities to realign with your soul's purpose. Rather than seeing disappointments or frustrations as blocks, consider them as reflective moments for introspection and recalibration. For example, when a planned venture doesn't proceed as expected, reassess your inner truth and ask if it truly aligns with you instead of dwelling on the stagnation. This may be your highest self prompting you to pause and consider these questions, an invitation to understand how unexpected obstacles are hidden blessings, providing clarity and direction you might not have considered otherwise. This reversed card is a gentle reminder that every detour or delay has the potential to guide you closer to a more authentic and fulfilling journey. Divine timing isn't external timing; it's a reflection of your internal readiness, reflected by the outer world.

Reflection

How can I use recent setbacks as opportunities to reassess my path and realign with what truly matters to me?

Four of Wands

Embrace the joy of completion and celebrate abundance with community.

Celebration, community, harmony, abundance, completion, homecoming, achievement

You have reached the end of a cycle. The *Four of Wands* shows how all your hard work and efforts are finally paying off, and it's now time to celebrate with those who have supported you along the way. Be grateful for all the blessings in your life and acknowledge the interconnectedness of all things. In this moment of renewal and happiness, come home to yourself and bask in the light of your achievements. Success is not a solitary endeavour and requires the collaboration of others, so celebrate with your community and honour the relationships that helped you reach this point. Look forward to what magic the future holds as you begin a new cycle or chapter in your life. Trust in your ability to manifest and shape your reality and move ahead with a deep sense of purpose, gratitude, and joy.

Reflection

What accomplishments or milestones have I recently achieved that I can celebrate?

How can I express gratitude for the support and encouragement of those who have helped me reach this point?

Reversed

Address imbalances and conflicts to restore harmony and stability.

Disruption, instability, isolation, unfulfilment, disharmony, insecurity, friction

When this card appears reversed, it suggests disruptions, delays, or unresolved conflicts, reflecting deeper issues that need attention. If you're feeling unfulfilled or noticing friction in your relationships, use these experiences as mirrors to explore what might be out of balance within yourself. This is an opportunity for deep introspection and a call to reconnect with your innermost values and needs. By facing these challenges with honesty and courage, you open the door to healing and re-establishing a sense of harmony, community, and belonging. You have the power within you to overcome these challenges and restore stability in your life.

Reflection

What areas of my life currently feel imbalanced or in conflict, and how can I approach these issues constructively?

How can I reconnect with my inner needs and values to overcome feelings of isolation or insecurity?

Five of Wands

Harness the energy of competition to overcome obstacles.

Conflict, competition, disagreements, challenges, obstacles, struggle, opposition

The *Five of Wands* represents a time when conflict, competition, and tension arise in your life. Don't be discouraged. Embrace an assertive, competitive energy with a sense of love and compassion, staying grounded in your values and sense of self. When you encounter disagreements with others, approach them with an open heart and a willingness to understand their perspectives. Seek out opportunities for collaboration and compromise, finding unity and resolution amid conflict. By releasing grudges and embracing the spirit of cooperation, you create harmony and understanding that supports you on your journey and them on theirs. Trust your ability to navigate through the challenges with grace and resilience, emerging stronger and wiser than ever before.

Reflection

Am I open to collaboration and compromise, or do I tend to be rigid and uncompromising in my views?

How can I cultivate a spirit of openness and flexibility in my interactions with others?

Can I use the energy of competition to push myself towards greater achievements while still maintaining a sense of balance and perspective?

Reversed

Find harmony through understanding and collaboration.

Resolution, harmony, unity, collaboration, agreement, cooperation, reconciliation

The *Five of Wands* reversed suggests that external disagreements mirror your inner conflicts and unresolved issues. In situations marked by conflict or competition, cultivate harmony through understanding and collaboration. Acknowledge and take responsibility for what's happening for you internally before trying to 'fix' the issue 'out there'. Remember also the significance of maintaining your boundaries. While exploring your inner conflicts, recognise the value of asserting your needs and limits. Approach conflicts with the intention of resolution and unity, but not at the expense of your wellbeing. Welcome dialogue, striving to understand diverse viewpoints while firmly upholding your personal boundaries. By balancing cooperation with self-care, you pave the way for healthier, more respectful interactions and relationships. Discord is simply a reminder of the importance of empathy and clear boundaries, fostering a community where every voice is heard and personal spaces are honoured.

Reflection

What steps can I take to promote cooperation and harmony in my interactions with others?

In what ways can I use my experiences of competition or disagreement as opportunities for personal growth and improved collaboration?

Six of Wands

Bask in the glory of your success and let your heart soar.

Triumph, success, achievement, recognition, honour, celebration, public acclaim

The *Six of Wands* signifies great achievement and success in your life, and you should be proud of all you have accomplished! Take a moment to bask in the glory of your achievements and celebrate your victories because you have proven you are capable of great things. Sometimes, success can cause your ego to become inflated, but staying grounded and true to your values keeps this in check. When you encounter setbacks or criticism, see them as another perspective and stay on your unique path. With your inner strength and resilience, you can overcome any obstacle and achieve whatever you choose. Take a deep breath, regroup, and continue moving forward with love, grace, and courage.

Reflection

What accomplishments am I most proud of, and how have they contributed to my personal growth?

How can I continue to grow and evolve, even after achieving a significant milestone or goal?

How can I use my success to inspire and uplift others around me?

Reversed

Believe in yourself and honour your unique path with pride.

Ego, pride, humiliation, setbacks, failure, disappointment, criticism, jealousy

The period represented by this reversed card is about looking inward and reaffirming your self-worth, not being dependent on external validation or acclaim. When experiencing disappointment or receiving negative feedback, view these moments as reflections of your inner strength and resilience. They are reminders to stay true to your values and vision, irrespective of external recognition. True success is measured by how well you align with your personal goals and values, not by public acclaim. Embrace feelings of failure or humiliation as opportunities for growth and self-discovery, and continue to move forward with humility and self-compassion, knowing that each experience enriches your journey and adds to your unique story.

Reflection

How can I maintain self-belief and confidence in the face of setbacks or criticism?

What lessons can experiences of failure or disappointment teach me, and how can they contribute to my growth?

In what ways can I stay committed to my path and values, regardless of external recognition or the jealousy of others?

Seven of Wands

Stand your ground and overcome obstacles with courage.

Boundaries, bravery, protection, challenge, perseverance, self-preservation

In the ever-shifting landscapes of life, the *Seven of Wands* asks you to stand tall amidst the tumultuous tides of adversity. Harness the unyielding spirit of the Wands, using their flames to ignite the embers of determination within your soul. Challenges, like waves, only serve to strengthen and refine the essence of your being. With unwavering courage and resilience, you shall rise above the fray, transforming the disarray into a triumphant tapestry. The battles you face are a testament to your growth, not an impediment to your journey. Rejoice in your inner growth, and let the wisdom gained from overcoming adversity illuminate your path, empowering you to ascend to the heights of your boundless potential.

Reflection

How can I use the lessons learned from past adversities to empower my personal growth and self-discovery?

In what ways can I transform the obstacles I encounter into opportunities for growth and positive change?

How can I celebrate my growth, both big and small, to cultivate a mindset of gratitude and motivation?

Reversed

Release the need to defend, and embrace vulnerability for growth.

Surrender, vulnerability, defeat, overwhelm, submission, giving up, intimidation

This card reversed indicates feelings of surrender, overwhelm, or defeat, yet these emotions are transformative when met with self-compassion. Instead of seeing submission as a weakness, view it as an opportunity for learning and growth. Being vulnerable means opening yourself up to new perspectives and experiences and moving away from the need to shield your emotions constantly. Consider this defensive stance as a barrier that prevents both you and others from seeing your authentic self. Making this shift can lead to a deeper self-understanding and foster more genuine connections with others. The reversed *Seven of Wands* invites you to let go of the struggle, accept help, and embrace change. These acts of bravery are important steps on your journey towards self-discovery.

Reflection

In what situations might letting down my guard and embracing vulnerability lead to personal growth?

How can accepting defeat or overwhelm in certain areas of my life open doors to new opportunities and learning experiences?

Can I practise self-compassion during times of surrender or submission, viewing them as steps towards a more authentic self?

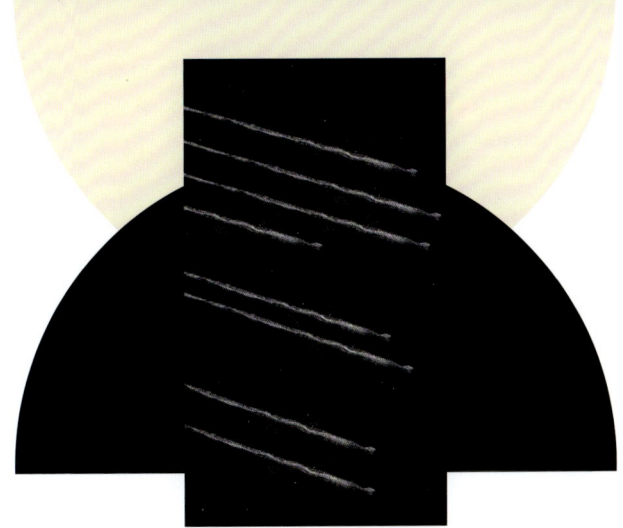

Eight of Wands

Harness the energy of momentum and propel forwards into limitless possibilities.

Speed, action, momentum, communication, swift movement, change, energy

The *Eight of Wands* signifies rapid movement, momentum, and swift change, urging you to seize the opportunities that come with this surge of energy. As you journey through life's ever-changing tides, speed and momentum are powerful allies, propelling you towards your highest aspirations. The energy of focused intention surges through your very essence. Embrace this kinetic force as an opportunity to soar, transcending limitations and achieving the unimaginable. Swift communication and decisive action unlock doors to boundless possibilities. In moments of doubt or hesitation, be guided by your heart and let the energy of progress guide you, illuminating your path to success.

Reflection

Can I harness the energy of speed and momentum to propel myself towards my goals and aspirations?

In what way can I use my energy and resources more efficiently to maintain forward momentum?

How can I effectively manage change and channel its power to create positive outcomes in my life?

Reversed

Navigate obstacles with clear communication to regain momentum and clarity.

Resistance, delays, frustration, obstacles, procrastination, distractions, slowing

When faced with resistance, delays, or frustrations, this reversed card encourages a calm and measured approach. Clear communication, both with yourself and others, becomes essential in understanding and overcoming any hurdles. Slowing down provides valuable insight, giving your truth time to emerge and allowing you to reassess your strategies and realign. This period of apparent slowing is not a setback but a chance to gather your thoughts and energies, ensuring that when you move forward again, it is with greater purpose and clarity. The reversed *Eight of Wands* reminds you how every obstacle is an invitation to grow stronger and more determined in pursuing your goals.

Reflection

How can clear communication help me navigate through current obstacles and regain momentum?

In what ways can a period of slowing down provide valuable insights for my path?

How can I turn current frustrations or delays into opportunities for refocusing and realignment with my goals?

Nine of Wands

Rise, resilient warrior, as victory awaits you.

Resilience, endurance, perseverance, fatigue, strength, stamina, determination

The *Nine of Wands* illustrates that you possess the unwavering spirit of a warrior even though you may often feel besieged by obstacles on life's arduous journey. Embrace these challenges, for they are the forge that tempers your resilience and resolve. Stand strong in the face of adversity, knowing your dreams and aspirations are worth protecting. Trust your innate fortitude, and let it guide you towards the triumph awaiting just beyond the horizon. Harness your invincible spirit and march forward with unwavering determination. Rise up and conquer the difficulties,

paving the way to your success. Let your heart's resilience and passion be your compass, guiding you to fulfil your dreams.
The world awaits your greatness. Seize the opportunity and claim your hard-earned victory.

Reflection

How can I tap into my inner resilience to turn challenges into opportunities for growth?

What strategies can I develop to manage stress and maintain my wellbeing effectively during difficult times?

How might I draw from my past experiences to cultivate courage and determination in the face of obstacles?

Reversed

Discover your inner power and persist with determination.

Doubt, exhaustion, hesitation, paranoia, insecurity, burnout, giving up, vulnerability

This reversed card signals that feeling hesitant and insecure is natural and offers valuable insights into your inner strength and resilience. When you face moments of burnout or feel like giving up, reflect on your true capabilities and untapped potential. This is a time for introspection and self-care, to recharge your spirit and renew your perspective. Embrace vulnerability as a source of power, allowing it to teach you how to set healthy boundaries and recognise your limits. Acknowledge your feelings of doubt or exhaustion and address them with compassion, paving the way for a resurgence of energy and a renewed commitment to your goals. Find the balance between perseverance and self-care, guiding you towards a sustainable path to achieving your aspirations.

Reflection

How can I embrace and learn from my doubt or exhaustion to strengthen my inner resilience?

How can acknowledging and working with my vulnerabilities lead to greater determination and a renewed sense of purpose?

What steps can I take to prioritise self-care and avoid burnout while continuing to pursue my goals?

Ten of Wands

Listen to your body's cues and set healthy boundaries and goals.

Burdens, responsibility, overload, stress, commitment, perseverance, hard work

This card reflects the weight of your commitments and the challenges that may feel overwhelming at times, but with mindful care, you can manage them with grace. As you walk the path of life, carrying the dreams and responsibilities that shape your journey, remember the deep well of strength and resilience within you. Each challenge offers you valuable wisdom, refining your character and expanding your understanding of the world. It's okay to ask for help and share the load when it feels too heavy. With unwavering determination and a clear vision, you will reach the heights you've worked so hard for, reaping the rewards of your dedication. Even when the burdens seem great, the *Ten of Wands* lovingly reminds you that you have the capacity to rise above and thrive. Move forward on your journey with passion and grace, knowing you are inspiring others as you pursue the life you envision.

Reflection

How can I maintain balance and wellbeing while managing my responsibilities?

In what areas of my life can I delegate tasks or seek support to lighten my load?

What strategies can I adopt to prioritise tasks and set realistic goals for myself?

Reversed

Release burdens by delegating wisely and prioritising self-care.

Delegation, release, learning, prioritising, unburdening, saying no, listening

The *Ten of Wands* reversed suggests re-evaluating your workload and responsibilities, understanding the importance of saying "no" and setting realistic boundaries for yourself. Listen to your body and mind, and heed their signals for rest and recuperation. Carrying too much alone leads to exhaustion and stress, and there is strength in acknowledging this and seeking support and sharing responsibilities. This reversed card encourages you to learn the art of prioritisation, unburdening yourself from unnecessary weights. By focusing on what truly matters and allowing others to assist, you create space for personal growth and wellbeing. Your journey need not be a solitary struggle; through wise delegation and self-care, you navigate your path with grace and ease.

Reflection

How can I identify and release tasks that overwhelm me and seek help where needed?

In what ways can prioritising self-care improve my ability to manage responsibilities?

What steps can I take to ensure I'm not taking on more than I can handle, and how can I effectively delegate to ease my load?

Page of Wands

Follow your curiosity, and let enthusiasm fuel your creative journey.

Exploration, enthusiasm, curiosity, adventure, inspiration, optimism, passion

This card signifies a time of exploration and boundless curiosity, inviting you to follow your passions with optimism and confidence. In the pursuit of your dreams, let your inner spark ignite your heart flame of passion and creativity. Embrace the spirit of adventure, daring to venture into uncharted territories with boundless enthusiasm and drive. As you forge your path, allow curiosity to guide you, discovering new possibilities and limitless potentials. Maintain an optimistic outlook, believing in your unique abilities and strengths. Remember, personal growth and transformation are yours for the taking as you harness the power of your own self-confidence and inspired vision.

Reflection

How can I cultivate a sense of curiosity and enthusiasm for learning and self-discovery?

In what areas of my life can I explore new opportunities through playfulness and curiosity?

What passions or interests have I been hesitant to pursue, and how can I overcome this?

Reversed

Overcome procrastination and self-doubt by focusing on your passions.

Hesitation, procrastination, insecurity, distraction, self-doubt, frustration, impatience

This card in reverse reflects moments where insecurities or distractions impede your creative journey, so delve deeper into what truly inspires and excites you. Re-evaluate where your energy is being directed and redirect it towards activities and goals that genuinely ignite your spirit. Confront feelings of self-doubt or frustration as opportunities to strengthen your resolve and realign with your true purpose. By reigniting your passion and dedication, you dissolve the barriers of procrastination and impatience. The reversed *Page of Wands* reminds you that your journey towards self-discovery is fuelled by your enthusiasm and commitment to pursue what truly matters to you.

Reflection

What specific passions or interests can reignite my enthusiasm and help me overcome procrastination?

How can I address and transform my feelings of insecurity or self-doubt into positive action?

In what ways can I rearrange my priorities to focus more on what truly inspires me?

Knight of Wands

Channel your passions and fearlessly pursue your dreams.

Action, energy, ambition, determination, fearlessness, boldness, confidence

The *Knight of Wands* encourages you to embrace your boundless energy and boldness, transforming your ambition into tangible action. Follow your dreams, allowing your charisma and inner strengths to light the way. Be mindful of the challenges ahead and be prepared to adapt and overcome obstacles with unwavering resolve and positivity. The true adventure lies not only in the destination but also in the exhilarating experience of growth and the pursuit of your highest aspirations. So, step forward with an open heart and fully embrace the journey that lies ahead. Go ahead and share your unique gifts and talents with the world, and let your passionate energy inspire others along the way.

Reflection

In what areas of my life can I cultivate more fearlessness through an open-minded and creative approach?

Can I balance my ambition with patience and thoughtful planning to ensure long-term success?

Can I step into my authentic self, using my innate gifts and talents to inspire and uplift others along my journey?

Reversed

*Balance your ambition with mindfulness
to achieve lasting success.*

Impatience, recklessness, haste, frustration, arrogance, domination, delays

The reversed *Knight of Wands* gently cautions you to be mindful of tendencies towards recklessness or impatience in your endeavours. Pause and thoughtfully reflect on your actions and their potential impacts. Rather than viewing moments of frustration or arrogance as obstacles, see them as valuable teachers guiding you towards cultivating patience and a more profound, thoughtful approach to life's journey. This is an opportunity for growth, inviting you to harmonise your vibrant drive and energy with mindfulness and consideration. True achievement flourishes from the harmonious blend of passion and wisdom, a dance of eagerness finely balanced with insight and foresight.

Reflection

How can I recognise and mitigate moments of impatience or recklessness in my pursuits?

What strategies can I employ to balance my ambition with mindful planning and patience?

In what ways can I channel my energy and enthusiasm into actions that are thoughtful, respectful, and aligned with my long-term goals?

Queen of Wands

Radiate confidence and warmth as you fearlessly pursue your potential.

Confidence, passion, warmth, courage, magnetism, optimism, independence, creativity

The *Queen of Wands*' message speaks of a powerful, creative force that radiates within you. This warm, magnetic energy draws others to you, giving you the potential to inspire and uplift them. Remember to balance your independence and determination with compassion and generosity towards others. Trust your instincts and have the courage to stand up for what you believe in, even in the face of challenges or opposition. Embrace your creativity and allow your unique voice to be heard, knowing that your influence can make a strong, positive impact on the world.

Reflection

How can I cultivate independence while also extending warmth and compassion to those around me?

In what ways can I use my powerful presence and magnetic energy to inspire and uplift those in my life?

How can I use my creativity to express my truths and make a meaningful contribution to the world?

Reversed

Reconnect with your inner wisdom to overcome doubt and regain clarity and compassion.

Selfishness, impatience, arrogance, jealousy, manipulation, insecurity, vengefulness, burnout

When the *Queen of Wands* appears reversed, it highlights moments of impatience, manipulation, or emotional insecurity that need to be addressed to regain balance and clarity. Reconnect with your inner wisdom to navigate through challenges and rediscover your clarity and compassion. In moments where impatience, arrogance, or insecurity arise, see these not as flaws but as signs calling you to deepen your self-awareness. They are beacons illuminating areas where you may have drifted from your inner truth. See this time as a chance to realign your approach, infusing your path with kindness, patience, and genuine understanding. This is a journey back to equilibrium, finding harmony between your needs and those of the world around you. Let the reversed *Queen of Wands* gently remind you that your greatest strength lies in your vulnerability and compassion. Reconnecting with these core qualities leads you back to a path filled with clarity and heartfelt purpose.

Reflection

How can I identify and address behaviours in myself that may be perceived as selfish or arrogant?

In what ways can I practise empathy and understanding to strengthen my relationships with others?

King of Wands

Follow your intuition and push forward with confidence.

Inspiration, passion, confidence, power, leader, entrepreneur, visionary

The *King of Wands* invites you to step into the role of a visionary leader, captivating and inspiring others with your unwavering enthusiasm and free-spirited ideas. Courage is your guiding star as you create your unique path, transcending limitations and seizing all opportunities. Recognise every challenge and triumph as a way to deepen your resilience and broaden your perspective. As you continue to evolve, your capacity to make a lasting, positive impact on others' lives only grows stronger. Rise up and take decisive action, harnessing your inner strengths and unique talents to turn your dreams into reality. Do not shy away from the greatness that resides within you; embrace yourself wholeheartedly and become all that you wish to be.

Reflection

What actions can I take to unleash my inner creativity and express it with confidence?

What practices can I adopt to ensure that I remain grounded, humble, and gracious as I navigate my leadership journey?

Reversed

Transform your weaknesses into strengths and lead with compassionate wisdom.

Impulsiveness, arrogance, domination, insecurity, recklessness, egotism, overconfidence, tyranny

This reversed card symbolises introspection on how traits like impulsiveness, arrogance, or overconfidence might mask underlying insecurities or fears. These characteristics are not fixed parts of your identity but signposts pointing towards areas for growth and self-improvement. Embrace a more balanced approach to leadership, one that combines self-assurance with humility and understanding. Reflect on how you can use your influence and power responsibly, leading in a way that uplifts and empowers others. True leadership stems from the heart — guiding with empathy, fairness, and a deep respect for yourself and those around you.

Reflection

In what way can I cultivate compassionate leadership, ensuring that I empower and inspire others rather than dominate?

How can embracing my vulnerabilities and insecurities enrich my ability to lead and connect with others more authentically?

About the Author

Sunshine Connelly was destined for a life of magic, connection, and wonder. Born in a rural village in the Philippines, she spent her early years immersed in nature with her psychic mother and surrounded by stories of other realms, including those of her great-grandfather, the village witch doctor. This rich heritage has fostered her deep connection with other dimensions, often channelling and connecting with otherworldly beings.

Now based in Melbourne, Australia, Sunshine is a designer, entrepreneur, and mum of three. She has founded and sold several startups across the technology, children's entertainment, and retail industries while also helping individuals discover their true selves through personal and business counselling and mentoring.

Sunshine believes that we are far more than our physical selves, and she is deeply passionate about sharing her visions and philosophies to guide others and elevate collective consciousness. Her works include the *Soul Mirror Oracle*, *Soul Mirror Journal*, and *Soul Reflections Tarot*, with her upcoming creation, *Oracle of Symbols*, featuring the captivating art of Ana Novaes.

Learn more at *sunshineconnelly.com*

About the Artist

Ana Novaes is a Brazilian artist based in São Paulo, active in the market since 2015 with publications worldwide, including *Soul Mirror Oracle*, *Nova Witch Tarot*, *Feminine Myths Oracle,* and *The Tarot of Secrets* with Blue Angel Publishing. She explores the collective unconscious through symbols and images that evoke dreams waiting to be deciphered. Her focus is on feminine figures, aiming to create and bring new perspectives and representations to these images, far from the male gaze. Novaes' creations exist between the conscious and unconscious worlds, between reality and dreams, establishing worlds we can explore with greater depth and without fear.

Learn more at *ananovaes.art*

More from Blue Angel Publishing®

The Baddeley Tarot
A Journey of Wisdom, Myth and Transformation

Jake Baddeley

The Baddeley Tarot invites you to explore an ancient system that has guided seekers for centuries, drawing upon the forbidden esoteric wisdom of the past. Hidden within the cards are the legends and myths of ancient times, now revealed in their full meaning and pattern, offering insight into the journey of the soul through life and beyond. Deeply researched and richly layered, this deck connects the symbolism of early tarots with the philosophies and spirit of the Renaissance era.

78 cards and 368-page colour guidebook.
ISBN: 978-1-922574-34-3

More from Blue Angel Publishing®

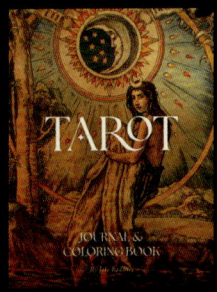 

Tarot Journal & Coloring Book

Jake Baddeley

The Tarot Journal & Coloring Book offers an immersive way to explore the tarot's deep symbolism and history. Featuring artwork from Jake Baddeley's acclaimed *The Baddeley Tarot* deck, this journal provides space for you to color the intricate illustrations and reflect on their meanings. Drawing from centuries-old tarot traditions and Renaissance influences, each image invites you to connect with timeless occult symbolism and mythologies. This journal is both a creative tool and a personal record, where you can capture your insights, interpretations, and reflections as you develop your understanding of the tarot.

220-page deluxe journal.

ISBN: 978-1-922574-28-2

More from Blue Angel Publishing®

Nova Witch Tarot
A deck for curious souls in search of magic

Suki Ferguson
Artwork by Ana Novaes

Nova Witch Tarot is a captivating deck tailored for young hearts and those new to tarot. These 78 cards and colour guidebook are your trusted allies, helping you dance through life's twists and turns with empathy and self-love. Illuminate the countless facets of your being while discovering hidden potential and unexpected paths into the future.

78 cards and 112-page colour guidebook.
ISBN: 978-1-922574-05-3

More from Blue Angel Publishing®

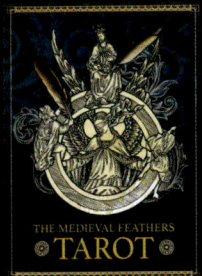

The Medieval Feathers Tarot
Messages From Heaven

Artwork & Concept by Alejandro R. Rozán
Text by Jay R. Rivera

In the realm of dreams, the boundaries of time are unclear, the hidden becomes seen, and desires can be welcomed into reality. Here, feathers of fate meld with medieval imagery, and profound insight unfolds in an elegant tapestry of self-reflection and divination. With layers of symbolism and nuance that pay homage to their antique predecessors, this exquisite set is a rich portal into understanding the intricacies of the Major and Minor Arcana.

80 cards and 232-page colour guidebook.
ISBN: 978-1-922573-89-6

More from Blue Angel Publishing®

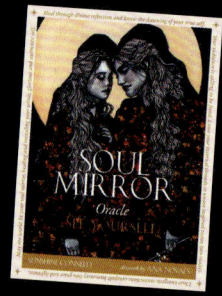

Soul Mirror Oracle
See Yourself

Sunshine Connelly
Artwork by Ana Novaes

Self-reflection is an active, ongoing, revealing and illuminating process. Within its light, you are freed into the understanding that we are all divine, all creators, all connected. Gaze into this oracle to transform fear, amplify love and welcome potent, tangible change. Embark on a spiritual odyssey of untangling the past, navigating shadows, bending energy and exquisite realisation.

42 cards and 120-page colour guidebook.
ISBN: 978-1-922573-85-8

More from Blue Angel Publishing®

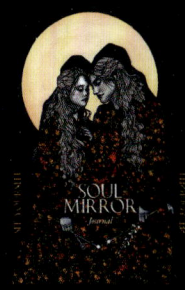

Soul Mirror Journal
Healing Through Divine Reflection

Sunshine Connelly
Artwork by Ana Novaes

Embark on your journalling odyssey as an homage to healing, truth and wholeness. With lined and unlined pages to encourage free expression, this is a unique space of personal recovery and discovery. Every inner knot you unravel is an opportunity to reweave the shining threads of your most authentic, ever-evolving self.

220-page deluxe journal.
ISBN: 978-1-922573-87-2

BLUE ANGEL
PUBLISHING

For more information on this or
any Blue Angel Publishing® release,
please visit our website at:

blueangelonline.com